Planned Assaults

The Nofamily House
Love/House
Texas Zero

Lars Lerup

Postscript by Peter Eisenman

Centre Canadien d'Architecture/
Canadian Centre for Architecture
Montréal

Distributed by The MIT Press
Cambridge, Massachusetts, and London, England

This book, designed by Eleanor Morris Caponigro, was set in Monotype Bembo and Gill Sans by Michael and Winifred Bixler and printed and bound by Meriden-Stinehour Press in the United States of America.

Library of Congress Cataloging in Publication Data

Lerup, Lars.
    Planned assaults.

    1. Housing, Single family. 2. Architecture, Domestic—Psychological aspects. 3. Communication in architectural design. 4. Architecture, Domestic—Designs and plans.   I. Title.

NA7125.L47   1987   728.3'7'01   86–23293
ISBN 0–262–62056–1 (paperback)
ISBN 0–262–12123–9 (hardcover)

Legal deposit: 2nd quarter, 1987
Bibliothèque nationale du Québec

Legal deposit: 2nd quarter, 1987
National Library of Canada

© 1987 Centre Canadien d'Architecture/Canadian Centre for Architecture

Contents

Acknowledgements   7
Foreword   Phyllis Lambert   9

Introduction   15
The Nofamily House   20
Love/House   59
Texas Zero   81

Postscript   Peter Eisenman   93

Sources   99
Figures and Plates   101

For Yngve Tegner and Harald Thafvelin

Acknowledgements

This book began over five years ago as a set of drawings of the Nofamily House, fragmentary notes, and long quotations from works on criticism and philosophy. It began its real life when the Canadian Centre for Architecture decided to acquire the Nofamily House drawings. Separate yet interwoven enterprises, drawing and writing happened almost simultaneously. Two additional projects, Love/House and Texas Zero, were added to the book in 1984.

I thank Anthony Vidler, Giorgio Ciucci, Anthony Dubovsky, Marc Treib, and Stanley Saitowitz for their valuable comments on the house projects. Foremost, I thank my friend and critic Peter Eisenman. His spirit and work, both written and architectural, have been an inspiration, and his comments on my work invaluable. I thank Jamileh Weber and Dolf Schnebli for their continual support of this project. I also thank Richard Ingersoll, Marc Eli Blanchard, and Josep Muntañola Thornberg for their insights and interest in my ideas.

I owe deepest thanks to Phyllis Lambert, Director of the Canadian Centre for Architecture, whose enthusiasm and commitment have made this project possible. CCA curator Eve Blau's toughness and unflagging demand for clarity made the book much better than it would otherwise have been. I cherish her commitment and friendship. Eleanor Caponigro's professionalism, wits, and wit made it a beautiful object. I thank Cynthia Ware for her editing of the final manuscript.

The Department of Architecture, University of California at Berkeley, granted a sabbatical to work on the book. The staff at the Institute for Architecture and Urban Studies in New York gave support in its initial stages.

The CCA funded the project and provided staff support for its completion.

Additionally, I thank Sylvia Russell for editorial help on earlier drafts, and Brett Bennett, Patrick Winters, Jeff Inaba, and Arturo Taboada for help with the illustrations. I thank Roger Conover of MIT Press for his spirited support and valuable comments. Finally, I thank Sohela Farokhi for her inspiration.

Lars Lerup

Foreword

The architectural investigations of Lars Lerup are both propositional and buildable, related both to the earliest published treatises on architecture and to post-Freudian theory.

As propositions, the three houses presented here belong to a contemporary phenomenon which has a long history as an architectural mode of thought, as an architectural genre. Stage and festival architecture are part of this tradition, as is architectural fantasy. There is also the class of building representation which proposes technologies not yet available. Finally, there are bodies of prints and drawings of buildings that are proposed as critical and philosophical discourse but are, like Lerup's houses, described in sufficient detail to permit imaginary walks through them. In these works the architect's intentionality is polemical and pedagogical: polemical in its critical view of society and demand for revision, pedagogical in its references to history and epistemology. It is here that Lerup's work is situated.

In *Planned Assaults* Lerup investigates three different houses. As their titles suggest, the houses are related to states of being rather than to the physical reality of use. The Nofamily House challenges the function and the accepted social and economic structures which engender the single-family house across North America. Lerup states the oppositions between the suburban tract house and architecture, all the while searching to join them by removing "family" to look at "house." Love/House explores the house as the locus of psychological relationships and the dialectic of dream and reality. Texas Zero begins at zero, 0-position, in assuming a program. It is more formal than narrative, at least in respect to the persona of the user, who

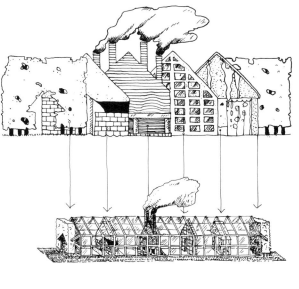

Villa Prima Facie: Greenhouse

also starts at 0-position. By conflating three generic Texas building types it posits the materiality of building and the tripartite form which are common to all three houses in this book, each representing a stage of "confrontation between House and Architecture."

Lerup's three buildings establish a typology of house, ordered in terms of structure (Texas Zero), use (Nofamily House), and perception (Love/House). These relationships constitute a sequential development when considered in the chronology of Lerup's work. In his first published house project, the Villa Prima Facie of 1978, Lerup sets out, as *poesis*, the fundamental structural element of the house, the wall: softwall, drywall, hotwall, hardwall, wetwall. A house of walls, Lerup writes in this publication, is "informed not by the primitive hut (Laugier), not by the machine (Le Corbusier), not by the city (Rossi) but by the single family house, the house that during the twentieth century has been the most prominent aspiration of my class." In Texas Zero Lerup goes back to the principal physical reality of replacing an archaic monolithic masonry with the North American tradition of skeleton frame and skin, or, in the terms he chooses for Texas Zero, the *ergon*, or the real work of the structure beneath, and

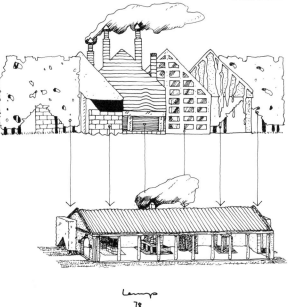

Villa Prima Facie: Palladian Shed

the *parergon*, or the by-work, the veil covering and separate from the real work.

Lerup's house typology is not one of tradition classified by location (city and country houses), or by class or income group. Rather, Lerup's typologies are research into other ways of thinking about *house*. Morphologically, however, Lerup's houses are traditional. Lerup starts from the same vernacular form that Sebastiano Serlio used in the sixteenth century—the child's drawing of a rectangular box with pitched roof—to construct a tripartite figure. The same symmetry obtains: the traditional *corps de logis*, or Lerup's "lump," expands into fact and figure, flanked by small rectangular boxes with pitched roofs, vestiges of vernacular origins, which have become service spaces. Perhaps the security of this form provides Lerup with a platform.

But his assault on the convention of the single-family house, while engaging the history of the house, demands serious attention to a modern state of being: the case of the isolated house in a society whose structures of thought, social interaction, and communication have nothing to do with classical certainties. He is, by contrast, interested in architecture as the formal expression of epistemological questions. Lerup makes planned assaults because he cannot make architecture out of the order of the day.

Lerup's text is an afterword drawn from the ideas that he develops in the process of drawing, and, from drawing to drawing, for each building with its proper concerns. Many models enter the work: the Beaux-Arts site-house plan, the Epinal child's cut-out, the work of contemporaries named by Lerup and others not named, the ideas of poets, philosophers, psychoanalysts. Every technique of drawing, every form of projection is investigated as if to wrest from them, and search through, all the possibilities of presentation and of the metaphysical state of building and occupant, the latter a subject discussed by Peter Eisenman in the postscript to the book.

For Lerup there is a consuming interest in the drawing as *œuvre* and statement. There are one hundred twenty-nine drawings for the Nofamily House. One hundred eighteen were acquired by the Canadian Centre for Architecture in 1981 as well as two models of the house. Lerup has since drawn other figures and views and generously added them to this group. The drawings were acquired as a corpus, consonant with the CCA's interest, as a study centre, in the way an architect thinks and develops ideas about buildings and communicates the results to client and builder, to teacher and student, to peers, to the general public.

This book, intended as one of a series of publications by the CCA on issues of contemporary architecture, brings Lerup's propositions to the attention of those concerned with architecture as a powerful expression of society and as a philosophical and public concern.

Phyllis Lambert
Director
Centre Canadien d'Architecture/
Canadian Centre for Architecture

Planned Assaults

Introduction

fig. 1   The Single-Family House: Figure and Plan

This work is an assault on the single-family house. Part exploration, part attack, part construction, part fiction. Your hand. The architect's hand.

The figure of the single-family house has two components. As in a child's drawing of a house, the figure is always seen from the outside. Although it is made up of parts (a rectangular box with a pitched roof, a chimney, windows, and a door), it appears solid, complete, closed off and therefore mute. Self-contained, it stands isolated in the suburban landscape. The totem of the American Dream.

Perpendicular to this vertical house figure lies the plan. An assembly of parts, the plan is a mere imprint that, with the help of labels, is given order and form: two-car garage, living and dining room, master bedroom, master bath, and the children's rooms. A graphic abstraction that can never be experienced directly, the plan is an unfolding affair, a journey in time: a promenade. Only as a drawing does it appear complete. Yet, like its vertical counterpart, the plan too is rigid and finite.

It is an interior landscape that we crisscross in our everyday lives. At the perimeter of this chain of elements is the outside world. The plan is the primary territory of the American Dream. Its syntax of spatial relationships is the master plan of the same dream.

A net of checks (rooms) and balances (doors), the plan forms the fundament of order and discipline for the family. Despite this obvious power over our lives, despite the incessant repetition of its syntax, the plan is taken for granted and is therefore experienced on the edge of our everyday consciousness. The rooms, doors, and windows are only stepping stones, objects of use.

Architecture has no place in this formula: The figure of the house and its plan serve as markers for the daily family narrative, to which architecture is related only peripherally. In order to bring architecture back onto centre stage, the flow of the narrative must be stopped or delayed. The introduction of architecture into the single-family house is therefore an assault on its stability, on its singularity of meaning as frame and vehicle—on its architectural muteness.

The Assault

This book describes three assaults on the single-family house and its dominating figure and plan, in the form of three house projects: The Nofamily House, the Love/House and the Texas Zero. They are an assault on the *world* of the single-family house, and as such are politically inspired. They assume a correspondence between political strategies and strategies of form. There is no attempt to convince the reader they are politically correct; persuasion is confined to the principles of architectural composition.

Underlying the work is thus the assumption that the single-family house is a "disciplinary mechanism"—morality manifested in form. The assignment of rooms, furniture, and equipment, and their syntax, is a vehicle of ideology and a behavioural modifier. The built form is supported by numerous additional structures of influence: the rhetoric of politics and law, ceremonial oratory, the language of everyday life, and various texts and image assemblies, from the codes of behaviour whose sources range from advice columns and advertising to television soap operas.

The reader must share with the architect some measure of agreement. On the meaning of the typical plan and its various components? Perhaps. To be a true accomplice, however, the reader must agree with the importance of interfering with the tyranny of the single-family house.

fig. 2   Gender Roles

Simultaneously, and at least as importantly, the houses are an aesthetic play on modernism and the general discipline of architecture—an orientation that has come to typify architecture in the postmodern era. It is perhaps this conscious undermining of dogma, be it modernism, historicism, or behaviourism, that is the most important inspiration in the work.

Transformation

The figure and the plan are static. A strategy is needed to animate them: the insertion of architecture.

A complex of three parts has been used in all three projects. This *tripartite figure* contains the principles for an architecture. It is a transformational principle—an architectural technology—in which two house figures and plans separated by a third form are transformed from one state to another, to produce a new house.

The notion of transformation is particularly prominent in modernism. Its origins are obscure; it is possible that the Beaux-Arts *marche* (the regimented route through a building) inspired Le Corbusier's concept of a *promenade architecturale* that in turn led to that of *mouvement architectural*, in which architecture itself rather than the pedestrian "moves" through a building. The current reinventors of transformation are the group of American modernists who gathered around Colin Rowe in the 1960s: John Hejduk, Robert Slutzky, and Peter Eisenman. The painting of Slutzky and the architecture of Eisenman have been particularly important.

The notion of transformation is, of course, much older. Architecture as transformation is about building, about itself, its own nature, its own mechanisms. Be it the void between column and wall, or the form between two houses, this in-between is the technology that transforms the elements of building into architecture.

Three Houses

The first project, the Nofamily House (1978–1982), disrupts the conventional house plan, with its living room, kitchen, master bedroom, and auxiliary bedrooms, in order to show that architecture represents itself and therefore also another aspect of ourselves. The assault on the figure of the house is direct. It is stripped bare to reveal its true emptiness. The resulting empty houses are separated by a lump of architecture. Two transparencies flank a solid: this is the tripartite figure. The opposition between the figures and the lump sets the stage for a confrontation between House and Architecture, between the family narrative and architecture's autonomy, between the language of use and the language of form.

The client for the Nofamily House is the family convention itself, the same crude fabrication that hovers in developers' and architects' minds. The automatons, or mannequins, of the family may be a cartoon, but most of us have to live in their footprints.

The second project, the Love/House (1981–1984) explores the hidden side of the single-family house—the place for love: the clandestine locus in the shadows of the city. An existing house is the desired object, which is transformed into the house for the waiting lover. A void separates the real house and the dream house and produces the tripartite figure. The transformation of the real into the dream is of Freudian inspiration. Not unlike the unconscious, the black, green, and white shadow-house stands as the other true reality against the convention of the single-family house. This other reality is architecture, in this case a mere dream and a drawing.

The client for the Love/House is the waiting lover who, be it ever so briefly, lives in all of us. The dream house, the scaffold of waiting, stands as an indictment of the single-family house, whose only trace of love is the master bed.

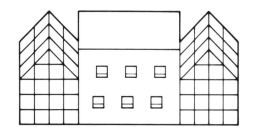

The Nofamily House

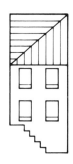

Love/House

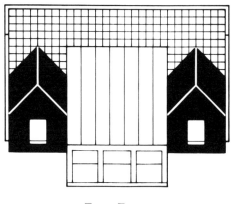

Texas Zero

fig. 3 The Tripartite Figures

The third project, the Texas Zero (1984), makes a new plan for an independent woman. The symbolic links among the conventional elements of the house are severed. A plan degree zero—value-free plane—empowers the inhabitant to develop her own domestic rituals, since the syntax of the conventional plan has been exchanged for a new order that reflects architecture rather than the family.

An almost found object, the Texas Zero is a hybrid of the typical house, a country store, and a log house, all characteristic buildings in the Texas landscape. The resulting tripartite figure is broken, however, allowing the family to slip out through its cracks and the client to breathe new life into the empty shell.

The strategy of the tripartite figure relies both on oppositions and correspondences. Its symmetry stands in contrast to the typical assymetry of the single-family house plan. Their collision sets the stage for new plans. This is the beginning; additonal strategies and associated figures must be added to bring them forth as full-fledged houses.

The Nofamily House

Erasure, Repetition, and Insertion

The first images of the Nofamily House are obscure. It is only in retrospect that a clear beginning emerges in two sources. One is the house as a generic figure of habitation through history, the most immediate example being the single-family house, with predecessors that include the Palladian Villa and Laugier's "primitive hut." In contrast to the mythic array of generic houses is the other source, the existing houses on the land. In Santa Cruz, California, the land, one hundred feet deep and six hundred feet long, reaches from a country road to a creek. Two houses occupy the first three hundred feet adjacent to the road. Here cultivation and habitation have been going on for some time. The remaining three hundred feet to the creek have stayed in the wild. Nature and culture — half of each. Myth and reality moved by a desire to make a new house. This is the beginning.

The reality: two existing houses and a garage. By the road, a blue one-room house stands in an overgrown garden next to a garage. Behind, at the edge of the wilderness, halfway to the creek, stands another house, also small and rudimentary but in complete disrepair. Two opposites: good and bad, new and old, prosperous and poor. But they are also connected since they are both houses: the fate of the new and prosperous may soon be that of the old and derelict. In this link is the beginning of an architectural transformation: the old house is *about* the new house, about the fate of houses in general. The process of material decay stands in contrast to the fixety of the figure of the house — like a child's drawing with its pitched roof, windows, door, and chimney — the discrete and potent symbol of the home,

fig. 4   The Shadows of the Single-family House: The Figure

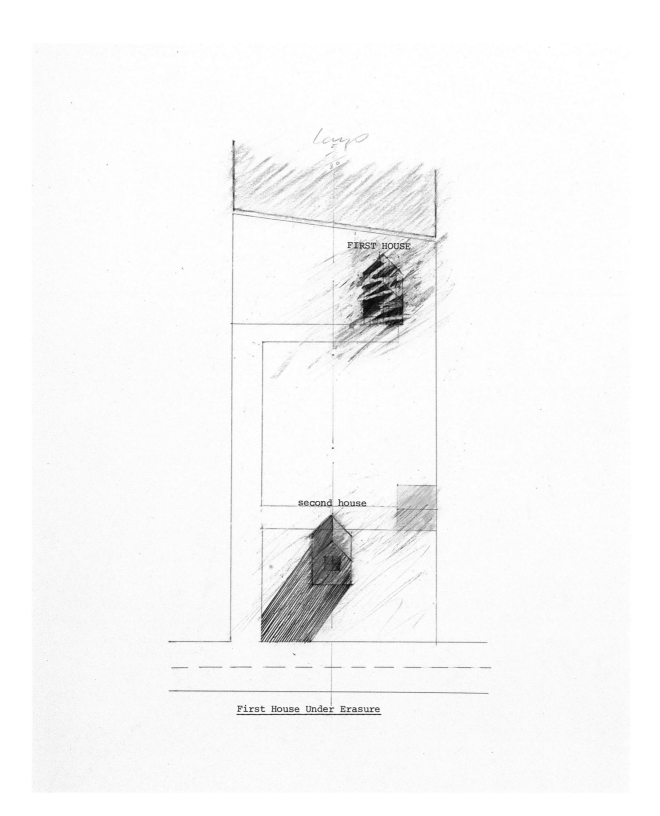

FIRST HOUSE

second house

First House Under Erasure

pl. I   The Erasure of the Derelict House

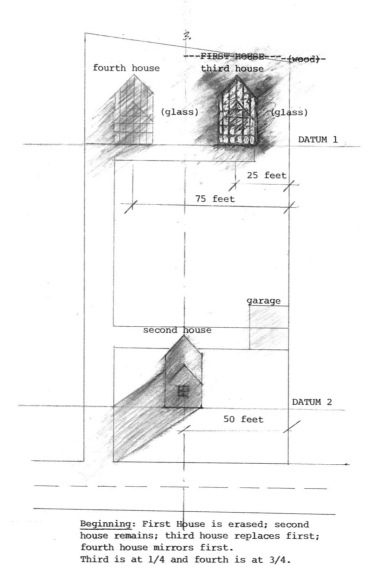

fourth house

third house

---FIRST HOUSE----(wood)-

(glass)   (glass)

DATUM 1

25 feet

75 feet

garage

second house

DATUM 2

50 feet

Beginning: First House is erased; second
house remains; third house replaces first;
fourth house mirrors first.
Third is at 1/4 and fourth is at 3/4.

pl. 2   The Glass House and Its Double

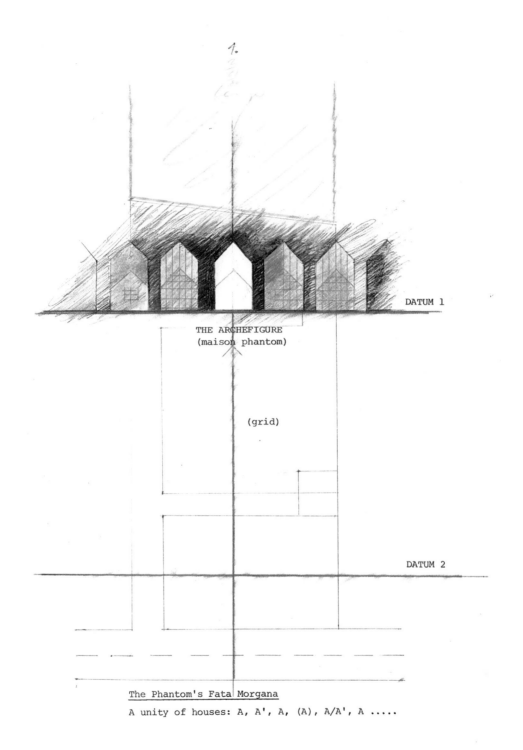

DATUM 1

THE ARCHEFIGURE
(maison phantom)

(grid)

DATUM 2

The Phantom's Fata Morgana

A unity of houses: A, A', A, (A), A/A', A .....

pl. 3   The Phantom's Fata Morgana or the Mad Swarming

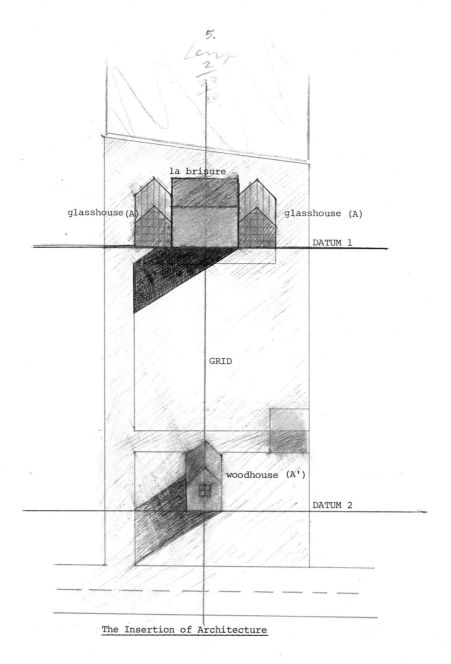

pl. 4   The Insertion of Architecture

the place of the family. This is the beginning: the mythic house is, through the figure, bonded to the real house.

The initial strategy is to erase the derelict house. A pragmatic as well as a symbolic act, this allows the old and decrepit house to fulfill its destiny and creates a clearing for a new house. This is the historical gesture. This gesture, however, is threatened by an array of houses from the past that, via memory, crowd the clearing: the historicist dilemma that the modernists refused to acknowledge.

In the clearing a new house is erected. But it is not completely new: it shares the outline — the rudiments of the figure — of the old house. As in a palimpsest, the old image of the house has been recovered. The erasure reveals rather than destroys. In it lie both the past and the future.

The new house is a thin metal structure covered by a grid of glass panes—the outline of a house. The old house has been stripped bare and reconstituted to reveal the figure in its complete emptiness. The new house is not designed but found in the gap between the old house and the life connoted by the word *house* (whose testament is the transparency of the glass house). The glass house is a mere sign of a house. Written in the figure of the glass house is a meaning far stronger than the mere sensory perception of an empty, almost invisible house.

Through the sign *house* flow its meanings: dwelling, home, family. This flow is diverted in the built sign of the house. The free flow of meaning is replaced by an abrupt swinging, back and forth, between what we see and what we read. The split between form and figure, between material and sign, is made apparent. The same object that promotes the idea of House simultaneously reveals its own form. The house glitters, reflects, rejects, and transforms the light that makes it visible to us: a prism, the empty house, the sign of the family, or simply a greenhouse.

The silent support is a complex matter that we know little about. It is unclear how the business of the family would change if the plan were completely erased. It is precisely this unclarity that makes these assaults viable.

A second glass house is constructed and placed symmetrically on the same datum as the first glass house. They are identical. Like beads on a string the figure suggests itself repeated across the landscape: the very image of suburbia with its repetition of garages, cars, husbands, hair dryers, and TV sets. This is the vast play of the family.

There is a curious contradiction between the apparent stability, the innocuous neutrality, of the two solitary glass houses and the possibility of their endless repetition. To avert this mad swarming, and to assault the tranquility of the house figures, a foreign element is inserted. The space between the signs — between the words — is occupied, seized. Architecture is inserted between the glass houses, momentarily to arrest the suburban repetition and expansion.

The yellow lump of architecture between the rudimentary houses is an unknown quantity. Inserted, it serves to divert the narrative of the family. A bridge as well as a break, the architectural lump allows by its contiguity a passing through — an architectural promenade — but simultaneously by its difference it rejects assimilation into the discourse of the single-family house. Architecture's autonomy. Solid and dense, the lump stands against the transparency of the glass houses.

The first phase of the making of the Nofamily House is accomplished. The tripartite figure is completed. The antagonism between what we read and what we see has been twice articulated: once, between the enigmatic presence of the glass houses and their historical and mythical doubles; second, between architecture as manifested in the yellow lump and the locus of the family as manifested in the glass houses. The collision between the two forces is yet to be accomplished.

Are your homes colonial style? This Carrier Year-round Weathermaker is one good practical answer. Place it in the basement, in a closet or in a utility room. Heating section is gas or oil fired. May be either water or air cooled. Occupies less than ten square feet.

Are your homes of contemporary design? Choose the Carrier air conditioning that suits your needs best. This combination is a Carrier Counterflow Winter Weathermaker with a Summer Weathermaker underneath. Refrigeration section is located outdoors.

fig. 5   Gender Space: Selling Air Conditioning in the 1950s

Zones of Passion

The conventional plan is the blueprint for the business of the family—the economics of love and fear. The glass house is the symbol of the blueprint. Through the blueprint, the family speaks.

The economy of space: The garage is as large as or larger than the living room, the boy's room is larger than the girls', beds grow wider with status and age, the master bath is larger than the family bath. The motor of the economy: the husband's work away, the housewifely tasks, the shopping (the eating), the games of power. The fear (child abuse, wife battering). The love (lovemaking, pleasures and joys, family festivities).

The spatial territories: The family makes its inscription on the plan (the family pictures, the memorabilia, the furniture, the vacuuming and dusting). Likewise, the family members cut the house into "man space," "woman space," "girl space," and "boy space." Within these domains, everyday activities inflict additional, if fleeting, spatial definitions (men cooking steaks, women cleaning, men doing dishes, girls playing house). These objects, lines, marks, gestures, and actions form a barely visible gender space (the true business environment of the family), silently supported by the plan.

The task of the yellow lump between the forceful glass houses is to maintain this enigma and to turn the spectator's attention constantly to its form and material. At first the lump is featureless, later characterized by front and back, inside and outside, up and down, facade, section, floor, ceiling, roof. But beyond these names lies the enigma of the surface, the plane, the hole, the break, the shift, the imbrications, the marks: an architectural bulwark against the desires, behaviours, gestures, plans, and narratives of the family.

The family could, of course, simply roll the blueprint of the single-family house plan across the surfaces of the lump, but in this particular and privileged theatre of form, the family must conform to the rules of the game. The complete territorial power of the family is translated into geometrical power in the world of the Nofamily House. Charged thus, the glass houses *rotate* and *shift* towards each other as, egocentrically, the family turns around itself, ruthlessly pursuing its narrative. This autoaffection is the rotation around two epicentres (one in each glass house). Further, the fecundity of the family, its tendency to repeat itself across the landscape to create an endless suburbia, a form of heteroaffection, causes the lateral shift in which the two glass houses attempt to meet and merge with one another.

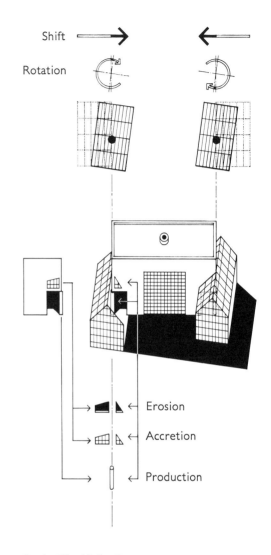

fig. 6   The Nofamily House: Zone of Passion

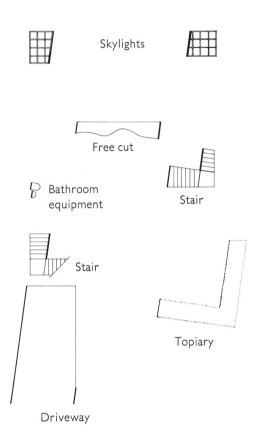

Skylights

Free cut

Bathroom equipment

Stair

Stair

Topiary

Driveway

fig. 7   The Nofamily House: Eight-Degree Fissures

The stubborn bulwark resists: speech arrested by silence.

This resistance creates zones of passion. The geometric turns and shifts are confronted by the solid, cement-block wall of the lump. Yet, before they succumb to the strength of the lump, each glass house rotates eight degrees and shifts a couple of feet: the architect's hand. The lump is affected, however; the rotating glass surfaces open gashes in it, but these cuts are in turn covered by glass blocks: the union of glass panes and cement block. A hollow column forms at each of the epicentres: marks of rotation, epicene, substitutes for the erosion of the load-bearing wall in the lump.

The transformation of the lump can be symbolized by rewriting the duality of figure and form as figure/form. Here the two are brought closer together and a symmetry is implied across the slash, yet their complete union is radically barred. The tilting bar holds, diverts, disrupts, and delays the flow of the graphic chain. As a graphic mark inscribed in this text, the slash is both the wall (in plan) and the column (in elevation). As text and drawing, the tripartite figure of the Nofamily House can be written: figure/form/figure.

The reverberations of the collision between house and architecture extend beyond the zones of passion. Like a seismic shock, the movements of the glass houses affect the various strata of the architectural ground. The rotation appears throughout the Nofamily House, in its stairs, in the direction of toilets and other bathroom fixtures, in the skylights, in the free cut between floors, in the driveway, in the topiary, and in the encounter between the deck of the house and the bordering wilderness of the site.

The relative and varying strength of the architectural ground is revealed in the fissures. Equipment such as toilets, shower stalls, bathtubs, sinks, and the kitchen counter is gathered in the zones of passion, as if calm can

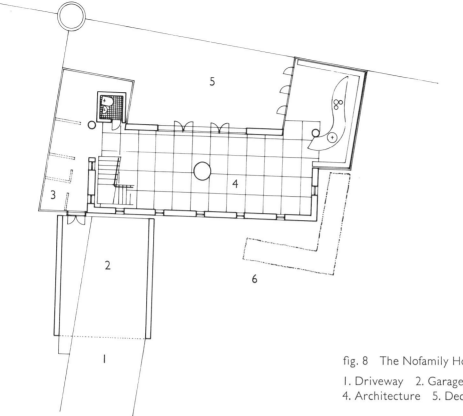

fig. 8   The Nofamily House: Plan I

1. Driveway   2. Garage   3. Glass house
4. Architecture   5. Deck   6. Topiary

be reached only in the epicentre. The topiary domesticated by the family shears, and the driveway, the path of the family car, both cohere with the glass houses, set against the walls of architecture.

The Plans

The plans of the Nofamily House appear quite logical at first, and indeed functionally they provide the necessities of life: shelter, kitchen equipment, bathroom equipment, stairs, some compartmentalization, and space to eat, sleep, and entertain. Architecturally there are, however, numerous complexities, as the Nofamily House is filled with expectations that are persistently frustrated.

Both floors in the lump are laid out on a typical modernist grid—a *plan libre*—a field of operation free of the de-

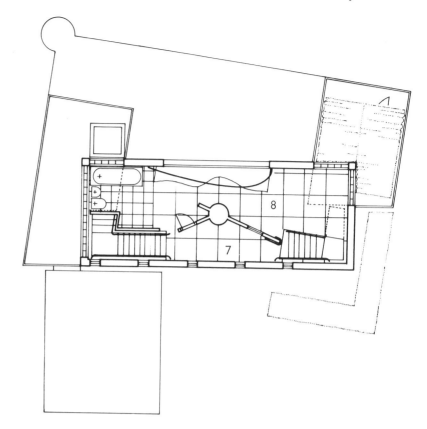

fig. 9   The Nofamily House: Plan 2
7. Hallway   8. Master bedroom

mands of the structure, which has been confined to the perimeter walls and the two columns. In the spirit of the free plan, a free cut in the second floor attempts also to create a free section. Stairs are located in the corners of the plan, and the bathroom fixtures are placed as objects in space. But across the free field two intersecting walls interrupt its flow. At the intersection of the cross, the hollow "column" of a fireplace is rammed through all the floors and the roof. As graphic marks, the cross and the spear occupy the centre of the plan, both defying the tenets of the free plan and making it impossible for the centre of the house to be occupied. Yet the crossing out of the free plan is not complete: one arm of the cross is missing; one is broken off. There is in these incomplete, frustrated formal strategies an uneasy union of opposites, symbolizing the limitations of dogma, of any dogma, and opening the doors on a wilderness.

Traps

Inscribed across the surfaces of the lump is another matrix of marks that serve to disrupt the narrative of the family. These disruptions deal directly with the intentions of the narrative as they appear in the single-family house plan, the functional promenade. The disruptions, or traps, are a way of dissecting the figure itself: of breaking it into elements to expose its inner mechanism. When does a functional promenade switch from being *for* the family to being *of* architecture? When does a functional element lose its name, a stair cease to be a narrative stepping stone and become an object of introspection? Never fully and always obscurely; yet to hover at the margin—at the slash in figure/form—is productive, since it is there that the inner workings of the architectural enterprise begin to be revealed.

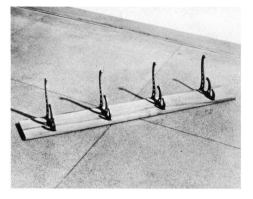

fig. 10   Duchamp's *Trébuchet*

The Nofamily House suggests, however, that a house ought to be a terra firma traversed by paths and checkered by domains of use, but intertwined with margins of wilderness in which *use* in the common sense is of little importance. Since the daily narratives are so all-consuming, however, and the dweller rarely pauses, traps must be inserted to expose the margins of the house.

The Liberated Handrail

Handrails, the epitome of narrative equipment, are among the most predictable fixtures found in the single-family house. They appear unobtrusively at each point or area where the dweller needs support, at a stair, or for protection from falling through an opening in the floor or a wall. Rarely do we give the handrail a glance as long as it satisfies our grasp. The handrail appears in the Nofamily House as expected, at one's fingertips at the bottom of the stairs on the first floor. On the second floor, however, the railings begin to move out of their logical domain; they still look like stair rails but the syntactic relationship with stair and hand is violated. High above the hand, as a connection

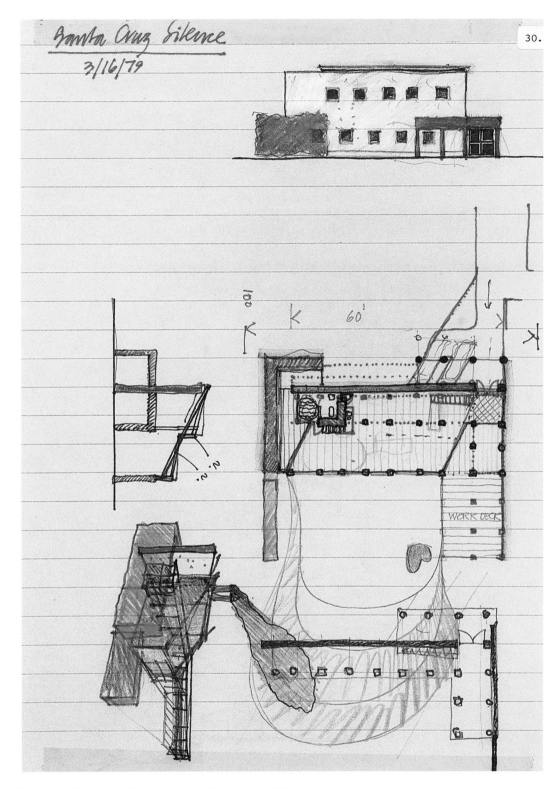

Santa Cruz Silence
3/16/79

30.

pl. 5   The Nofamily House: Sketch, Facade (Plan, Section, View)

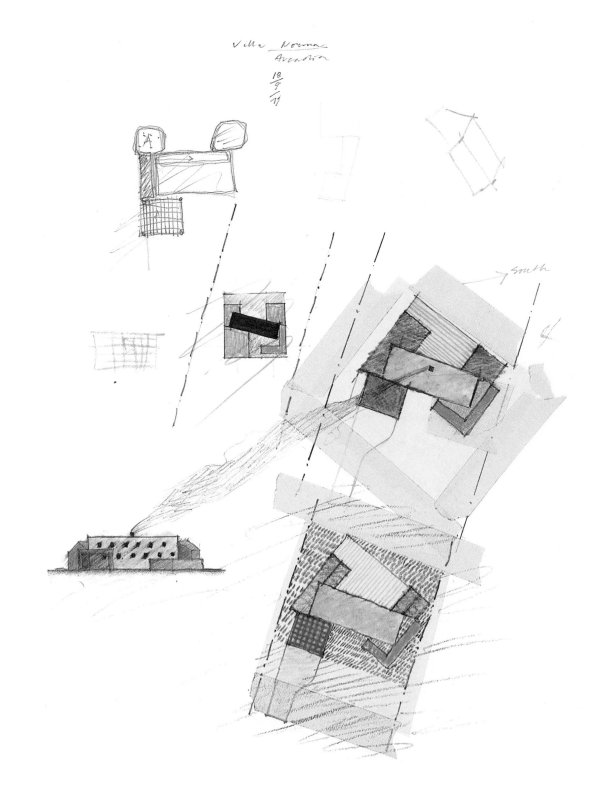

pl. 6   The Nofamily House: Sketch, First Rotation

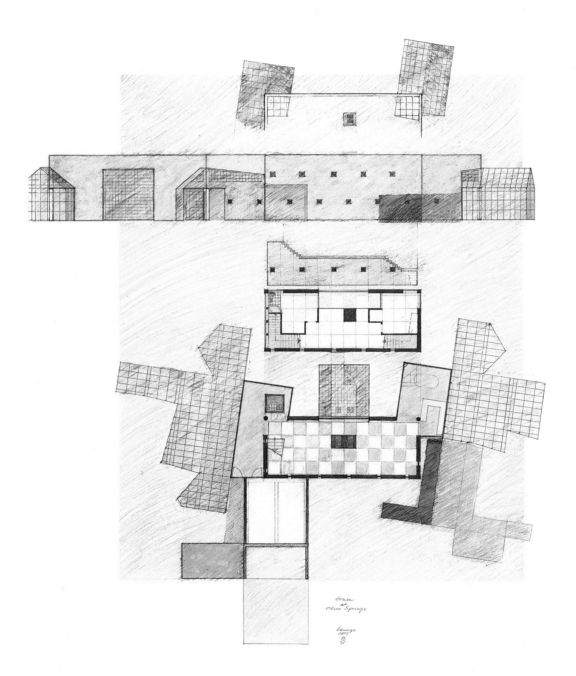

pl. 7   The Nofamily House: Preliminary Design, Fold-out View

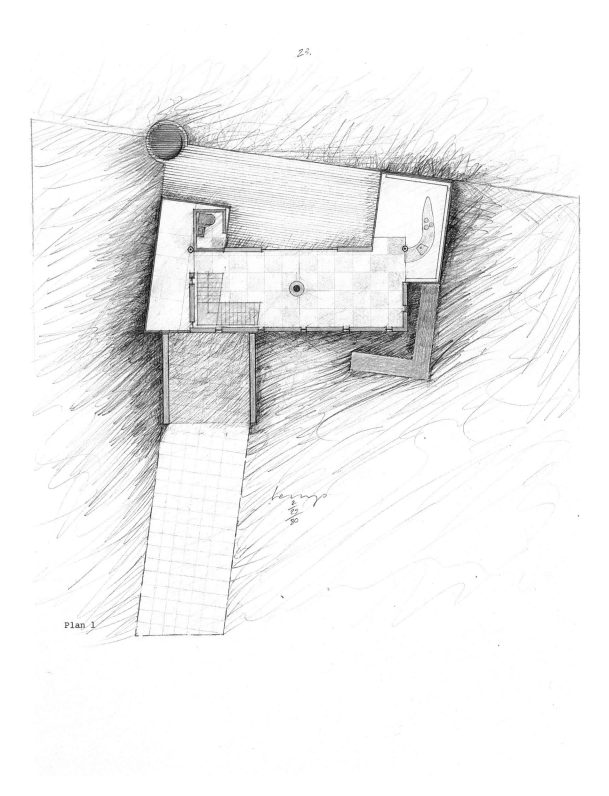

Plan 1

pl. 8   The Nofamily House: Plan I

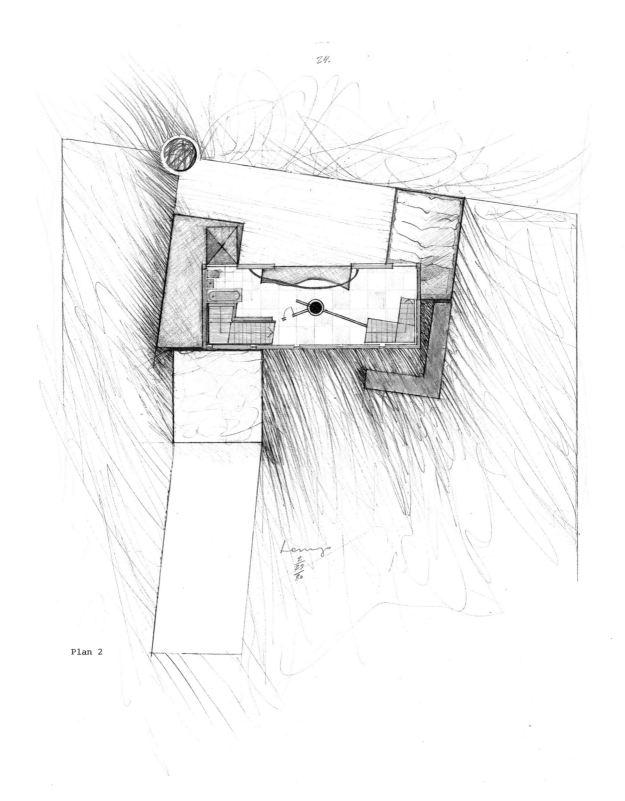

pl. 9   The Nofamily House: Plan 2

pl. 10   The Nofamily House: Roof Plan

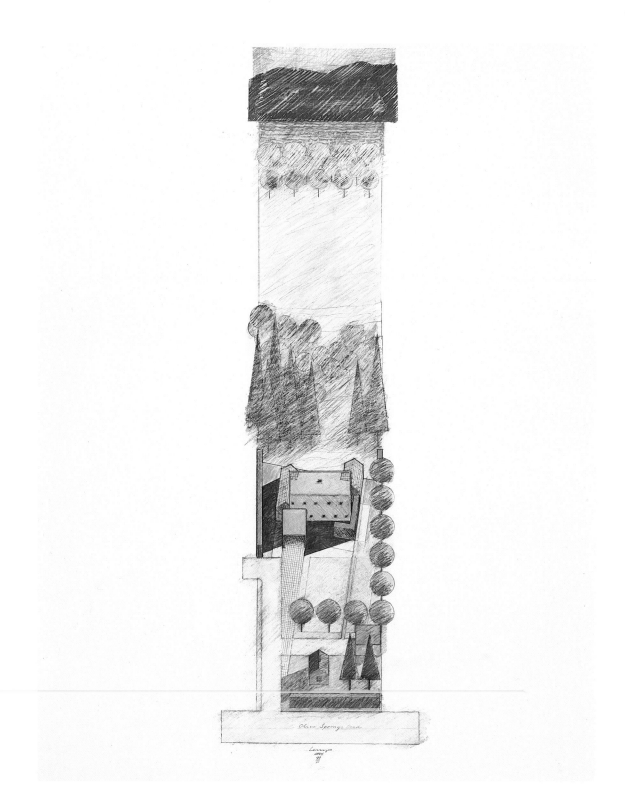

pl. 11   The Nofamily House: Site Plan

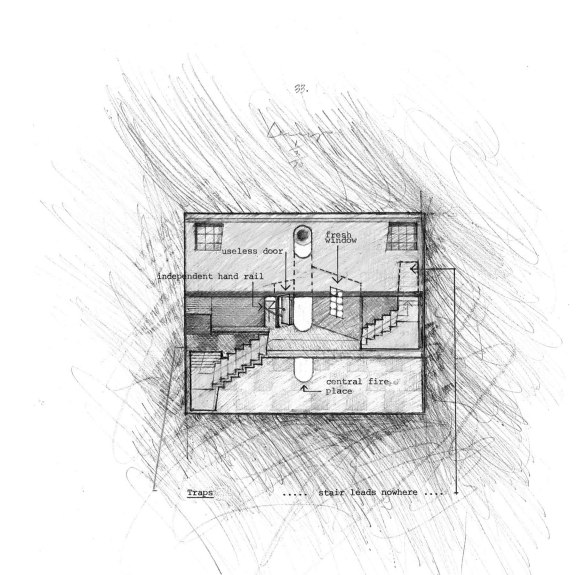

useless door

fresh window

independent hand rail

central fire place

Traps ..... stair leads nowhere ....

pl. 12   A Stumble of Traps: The Liberated Handrail, the Useless Door, the Fresh Window, the Stair That Leads Nowhere

The Liberated Handrail

pl. 13   The Liberated Handrail

pl. 14   The Useless Door

pl. 15   The Fresh Window

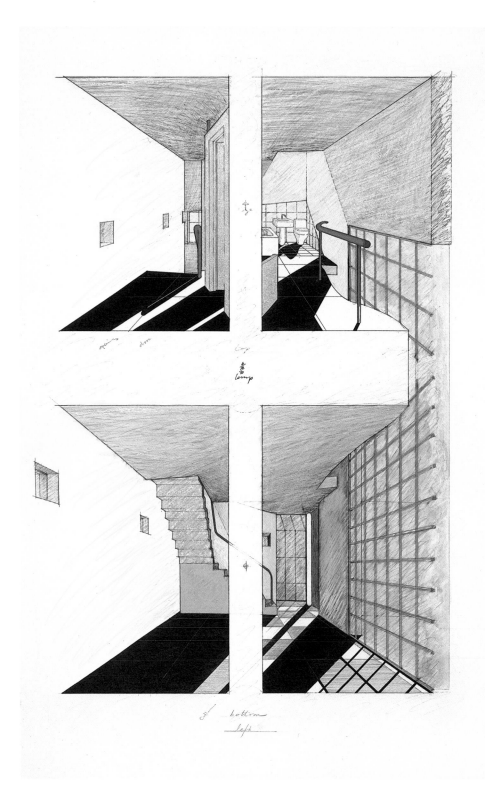

pl. 16   The Nofamily House: Interior Views; Perspective from Architecture's Point of View (Left)

pl. 17   The Nofamily House: Interior Views; Perspective from Architecture's Point of View (Right)

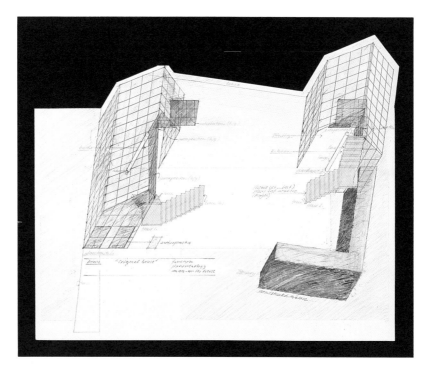

pl. 18a   The Nofamily House: Dissection; The Locus of the Family

pl. 18b   The Nofamily House: Dissection; The Locus of Architecture (Inside)

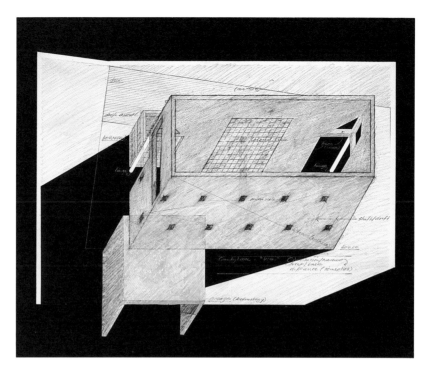

pl. 18c   The Nofamily House: Dissection; The Locus of Architecture (Outside)

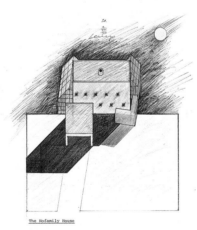

The Nofamily House

pl. 19   The Nofamily House: View

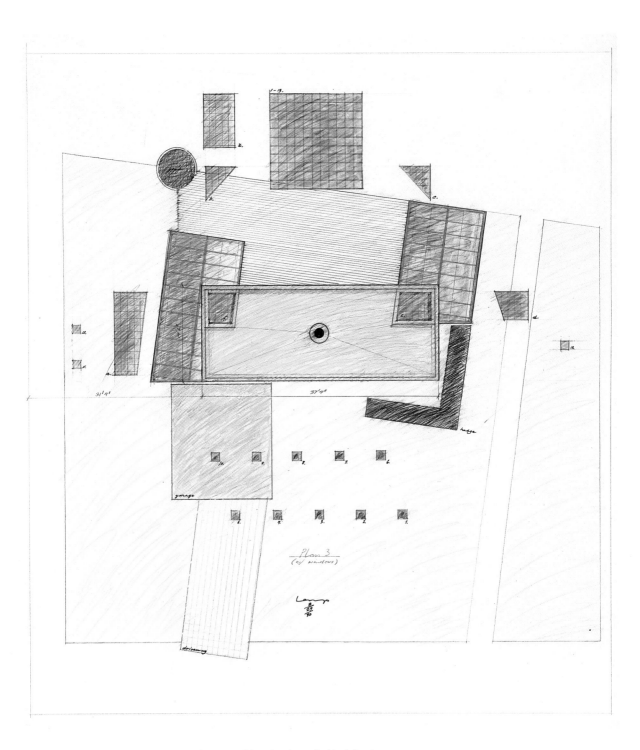

Plan 3
(w/ windows)

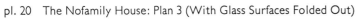

pl. 20   The Nofamily House: Plan 3 (With Glass Surfaces Folded Out)

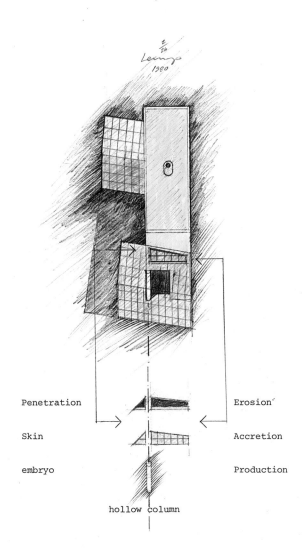

Penetration   Erosion

Skin   Accretion

embryo   Production

hollow column

Zone of Passion

pl. 21   Zone of Passion: Rotation and Shift

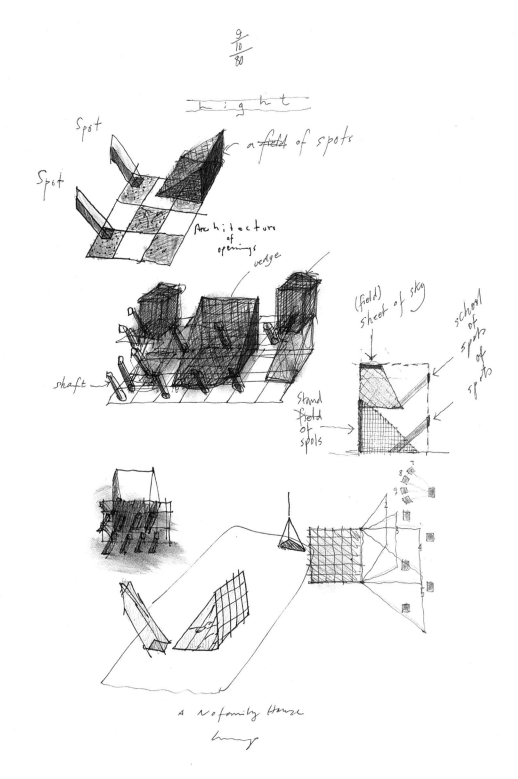

l i g h t

Spot

Spot

a field of spots

Architecture of openings

wedge

shaft

(field) sheet of sky

school of spots of spots

Stand field of spots

A No family House

pl. 22   Exploration: Shafts of Light

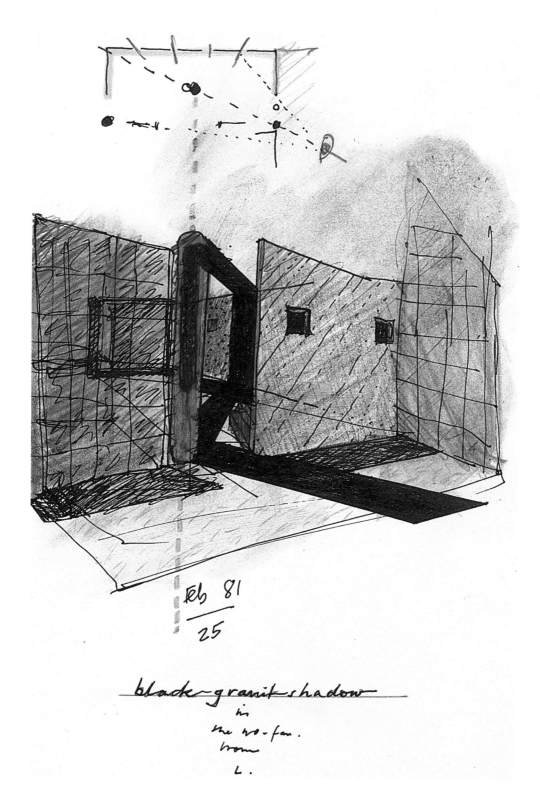

Feb 81
25

black granite shadow
in
the no-fan.
from
L.

pl. 23   Exploration: The Granite Shadow

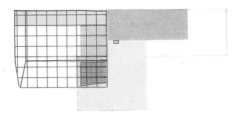

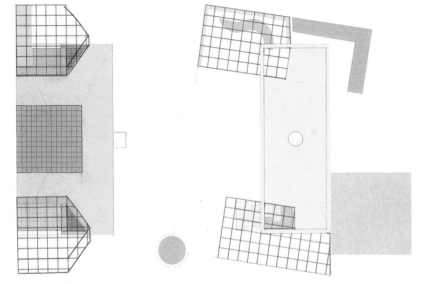

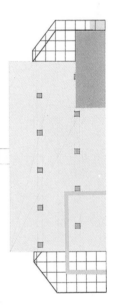

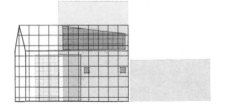

pl. 24   Foxtrot Collage: Roof Plan and Elevations

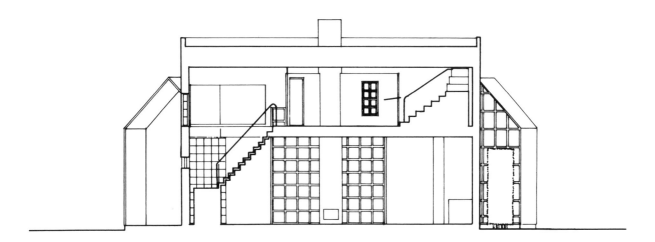

fig. 11   The Nofamily House: Section

between an abruptly terminated wall and the ceiling, a short piece of rail appears. At the free cut in the floor the railing has taken its own course, dangerously leaving the user's hand and foot uncoordinated, unsure of which to follow, railing or crevice. The handrail is no longer a safety device. The name *handrail* is momentarily separated from the object *handrail*. It is a trap, an independent agent on its own errand into an antifunctional wilderness.

The arbitrary connection between the word and the object is revealed; even the function is set adrift. The margins of narrative space are exposed. Somewhere between the domesticated handrail and the pure object is a ground that may very well be the archi-trace of space—the edge between civilization and wilderness whose metaphor is the slash in figure/form—a fleeting mark that admits to its narrative responsibility yet resists complete co-option.

The Liberated Handrail, the first of several traps set in the Nofamily House, borrows its logic from the dadaists. It is like the coatrack in Marcel Duchamp's *Trébuchet*, which becomes a trap when left on the floor, where its benevolent hooks are dangerous fangs ready to trip the unknowing pedestrian. The form appears between the hook and the fang, yet the figure never quite leaves. The connection between object, language, and human behaviour is fluid.

The Useless Door

At the top of the stairs on the second floor a door appears. Since it is placed next to an opening that allows free entry to the space beyond, the door is completely useless. Unlike its dadaist predecessor, Duchamp's door, which is both open and closed because it serves two perpendicular openings at the same time, this one has no function. Or can it, with hinges left unoiled, be used as a rudimentary musical instrument? Will it always be open or closed? Is it in fact a door? Or has it been forced down in the taxonomy, to a mere lump? Or up, to become a pure sign? Or perhaps, as Mallarmé writes, "What is speaking is the object itself in its own precarious being."

The Fresh Window

On the corresponding flared wall, next to the Useless Door, is a window. The window opens on what may become the master bedroom. Again the inspiration is Duchamp and his *Fresh Widow* of 1920 (a model of a French window, fitted with leather rather than glass panes, which he insisted should be polished every day like shoes).

The Nofamily House returns the small French window to its proper size and fits it with regular glass panes. But it has a tenuous relation to the family of windows: windows appear in exterior walls, the Fresh Window in an interior wall; windows are meant to be looked out of, not in through, as here. The Fresh Window threatens the domestic scene, making the Peeping Tom legitimate by letting him inside the house and placing him in the hallway, outside the bedroom: looking now, legitimately, out into the bedroom. In the shift from the taming to the liberation of the gaze—the turning of the French window inside out—the slash in figure/form flashes by, adrift, a non-site, the

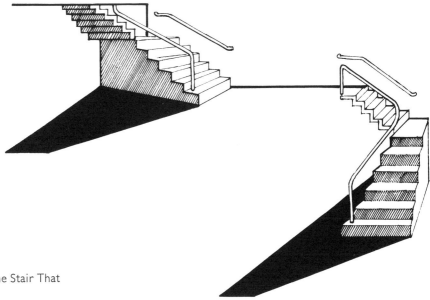

fig. 12 The Nofamily House: The Stair That
Leads Nowhere

place of architecture. An additional thought is given to
the window and a fresh viewpoint to the eye.

The Stair That Leads Nowhere

At the Fresh Window, a stair ascends and turns out of
sight. It is both inside the hallway and partially inside the
"bedroom." By climbing the stair, turning, and so de-
scending along the angle of its flare, it can be used to enter
the bedroom, making the Useless Door twice as useless.
Climbing the stair farther up under the ceiling reveals the
last of the traps: The Stair That Leads Nowhere.

The rhetorical figure of symmetry (one dogleg stair in
each corner of the lump) and repetition (two almost-
identical stairs) is disrupted. A reversion takes place: the
stair turns in on itself and, like a snake in springtime, peels
off its name. The hiatus between language and house with
all its elements is exposed by the heterogeneous stair. A
mere sign, the stair, like the window, the door, and the
handrail, has joined the wilderness beyond the domestic
narrative.

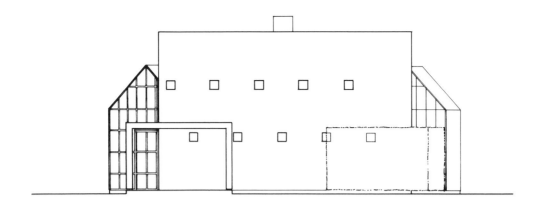

fig. 13   The Nofamily House: Front Facade (North)

The promenade has reached a sudden end. The return reveals again the expectation, the traps, and the frustration. The fixed smile of the single-family house with its two figures is broken. Like debris, fragments of house and architecture are imbricated, defying any complete readings and rejecting all dogma. The family is momentarily relieved of its task as ultimate referent.

Facades And Other Externalities

A blue house, a pink garage, two glass houses, and a rudely inserted yellow lump. The Nofamily House sits at the break between culture and nature. A wooden deck bridges the house; the back facade has a large picture window, with the wilderness beyond. The front facade, the elevation that faces the city, consists of a wall with an array of small square windows that wander across it in offset bands. The windows continue around the corner on both side facades. Added together (and squared) they equal the size of the picture window in the back. Repetition and agglomeration make a kind of automatic writing across the facades; there are no references to human use until you see the large window. Unlike the front picture window in the suburban house, this one faces nature rather than the street, an inversion that changes both meaning and use. The

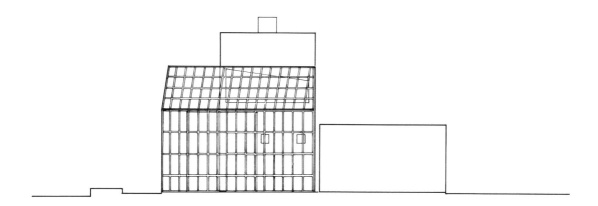

fig. 14   The Nofamily House: Side Facade (East)

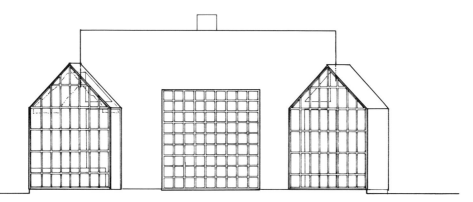

fig. 15   The Nofamily House: Back Facade (South)

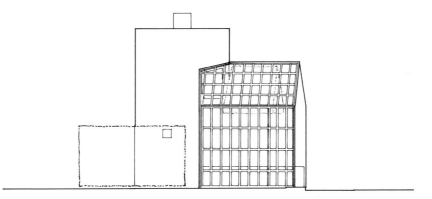

fig. 16   The Nofamily House: Side Facade (West)

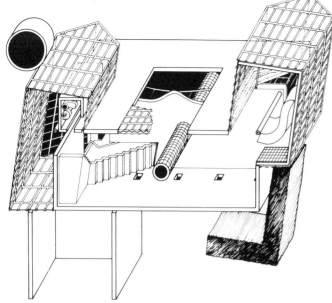

fig. 17   The Nofamily House: Axonometric from Under

facade is closed to the city and open to nature; the sun rather than the neighbour's gaze is invited into the house.

Predictably, the garage sits at the end of the long driveway, but entry is directly from the garage to the adjacent glass house. There is no front door in the front facade: use over convention.

Opposite the garage grows an angular topiary bush, suggesting a ruined wall of a real greenhouse or a thick shadow cast from the bordering glass house. At the edge of the deck a hot tub straddles civilization and nature, and concludes a series of hinges between house and nature.

The centre of the Nofamily House is taken up by the large white chimney, a giant version of the columns in the zones of passion. Again, the anthropomorphic trace occupies the centre of architecture. This is not the last, not the darkest shadow of the figure. The archaeology of the single-family house, with its master bedroom, the room for the oldest son, the room for the girls, is engraved on the black concrete floor in the glass house at the entry. Irreducible, figure inhabits form, as a row of columns inhabits a wall. This irreducibility is the great difficulty with architecture.

Love/House

Amorous Figures

The project is driven by a singular activity, a single emotion—waiting. A particular kind of waiting, that of waiting for the lover.

The single-family house has no space for lovers. Even the discourse of love must live a clandestine existence inside language. As secret figures, lovers must hide in the shadows of more prominent things of the city.

The rose-coloured house sits in the corner of the fourth and last court, deep inside a block in Paris. She lives in the house. Outside, he waits, in the deep shadow of her house.

He waits impatiently. Her house is silent. She is gone. The sun is gone. The shadow fills the court. He can hear the widow. The madman mutters to himself. Their respective houses form the entry to the court. Like guards, the lonely and the mad control the comings and goings in the lovers' court. To the right, behind a high wall, the schoolyard lies empty, waiting patiently for the voices of tomorrow's children. Putting his head to the back wall of the court, he can hear the foreign voices of immigrants at supper. Parallel to the school wall stands an even higher wall, now in complete darkness. Behind it lies the unknown, inhabited by darkness and stray cats. This is the reality.

If only the darkness of the court had a permanent thickness, he would have a place to wait. A place of his own. Suddenly, the artificial light is turned on. All four courts are flooded with light. Somebody has entered from the street. His momentary hiding place is gone.

This is one possible entry into the Lovers' Discourse. The single-family house has few if any entries. Even her house,

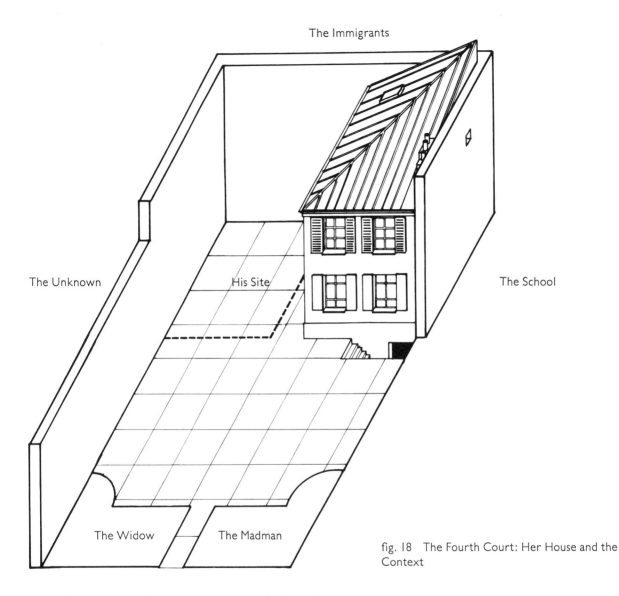

The Immigrants

The Unknown

His Site

The School

The Widow

The Madman

fig. 18   The Fourth Court: Her House and the Context

whose late-nineteenth-century layout crudely prefigures the ultimate compartmentalization of the modern family, has no entry or crevice for his waiting. Generally it is the public or semipublic margins of the city that give the lovers their brief shelter: cafés, restaurants, sidewalks, parks, courts, and the brief, purchased privacy of the hotel room. The fourth court in the depth of the city seems a natural place for the lovers' dream house.

pl. 25   Love/House: Site (City, District, House)

View of the Court

pl. 26   The Fourth Court

pl. 27 Scene: The Four Courts and the Eiffel Tower

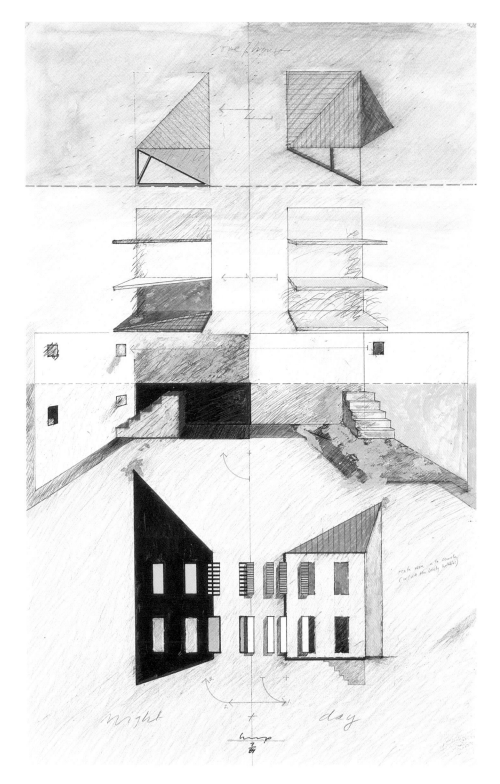

pl. 28   Love/House: Transformations (Night and Day)

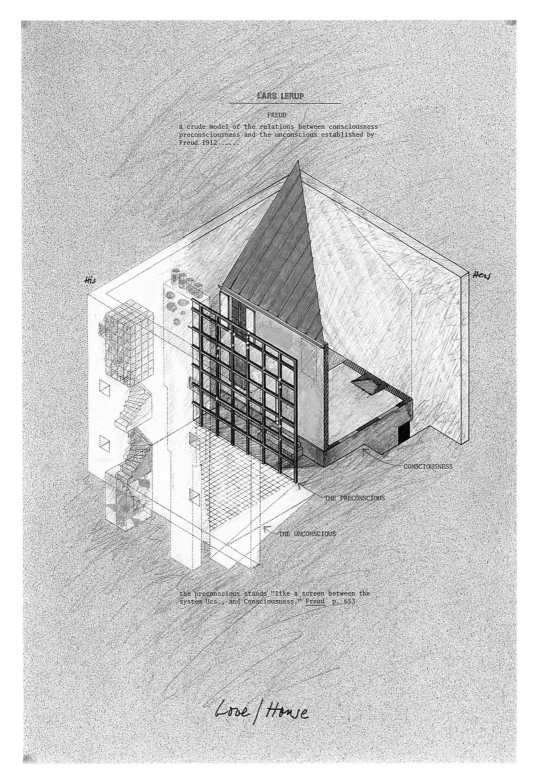

LARS LERUP

FREUD

a crude model of the relations between consciousness
preconsciousness and the unconscious established by
Freud 1912 . . . . .

His

Hers

CONSCIOUSNESS

THE PRECONSCIOUS

THE UNCONSCIOUS

the preconscious stands "like a screen between the
system Ucs., and Consciousness." Freud p. 653

Love / House

pl. 29   Freud's Dream Technology

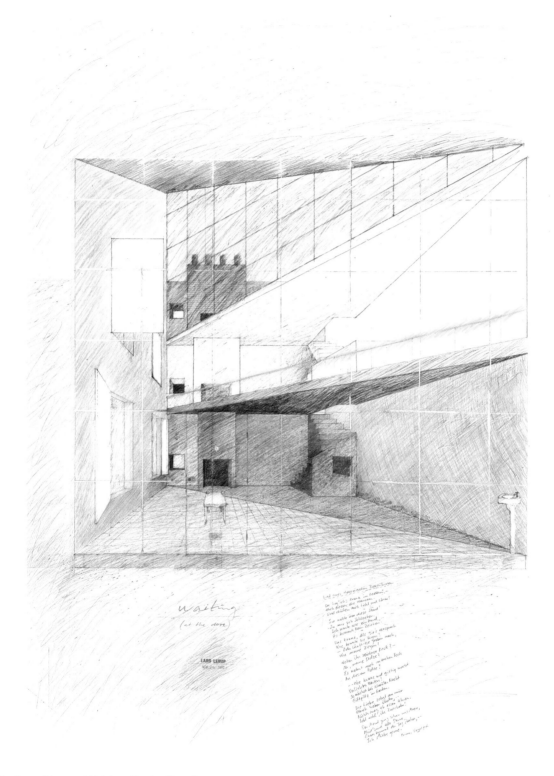

waiting

(at the door)

LARS LERUP

pl. 30   Love/House: Waiting (At the Door)

pl. 31   "Malicious Spying": From the Widow's Point of View

She used to part the curtain and peek through her window and look down into the court to see what the lovers were up to.

enigma
of the night

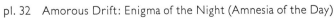

pl. 32   Amorous Drift: Enigma of the Night (Amnesia of the Day)

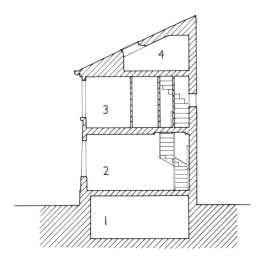

fig. 19   Her House: Section
1. Cellar   2. Kitchen/dining/living   3. Studio
4. Attic

Utterly simple, her house is a typical Parisian house, smaller than a palace, smaller than the buildings on the boulevard, but made up of the same elements. Her house is like a token, a model of an ideal house: cellar, a first floor with a fireplace and kitchen-living-dining room, a second-floor studio, and a third-floor attic where she sleeps. The front facade, with four windows and shutters, and the side facade, with a door, a kitchen window, and an upstairs window to the studio, complete the figure of the house. When she is gone, the house, as her token, remains. Her absence is its presence.

Standing opposite her house, with his back to the dark wall of the Unknown, facing her side facade, he begins to dream his house: She is the content of his dreams, her house the content of his house. She has left, nowhere to be found; her house is silent, abandoned to his worries, hopes, and fantasies. Open to his reading.

Slowly, her house becomes the armature for all the conventions of the Lovers' Discourse. Roland Barthes calls these figures a collection of "amorous figures," in which the word *figure* should be "understood not in its rhetorical sense, but rather in its gymnastic or choreographic acceptation; . . . the body's gesture caught in action and not contemplated in repose." The amorous figures are "outlined" in discourse, then become memorable and established when we exclaim, "That's so true! I recognize that scene of language." Yet they have no locus, no place in the house, only in the shadows of the city. Empty, her house becomes haunted by all lovers' collected figures, which, like bats and swallows, come to inhabit the windows, doors, rooms, and fabric of her house.

To fill her empty house with Barthes's discourse is the first step. An array of figures is fastened like speech bubbles in a cartoon through a set of correspondences to the wall that separates her house from his site. This Love Wall contains four architectural figures: the door, open or closed, the sign of her presence; a window with a grille, preventing forced entry to the kitchen behind; a window upstairs that she erased to make more wall space, and, next to it, a French window with shutters, a typical window in the city. The Love Wall with its figures becomes the site for Barthes's amorous figures.

The *French Window*, the ultimate symbol of the bourgeois gaze: Barthes's "Show Me Whom to Desire."

The body which will be loved is in advance selected and manipulated by the lens *subjected to a kind of* zoom effect *which magnifies it, brings it closer, and leads the subject to press his nose to the* glass*: is it not the scintillating object which the skillful hand causes to shimmer before me and which hypnotizes me, captures me?* (A Lovers' Discourse: Fragments)

Lens, zoom effect, nose to the glass: pure coincidence, but the French window shimmers between the lines. Other figures, "The Informer" and "Jealousy," hover here too.

The *Imprisoned Window* suggests yet others: "Dependency," "We Are Our Own Demons," "Love's Languor." "Such is amorous fatigue: a hunger not to be satisfied, a gaping love." At the Imprisoned Window, he stands unable to enter, unable to see through the grille. Behind it is the kitchen, her own and other women's collective prison. Kitchen, hunger, impassable grille—no longer just coincidence?

The *Erased Window*: "The Unknowable," "Atopos," "Dark Glasses," "No Answer." "The loved being becomes a leaden figure, a dream creature who does not speak, and silence, in dreams, in death." He gazes at the Erased Window, whose faint outlines suggest a window, but whose reality as solid wall also denies it. He cannot see her, only imagine her behind the leaden wall.

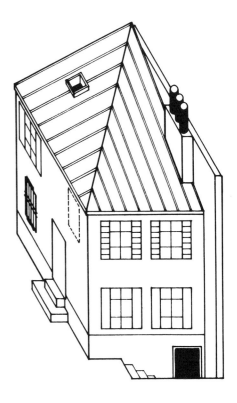

fig. 20　The Love Wall: The Locus of Barthes's Amorous Figures

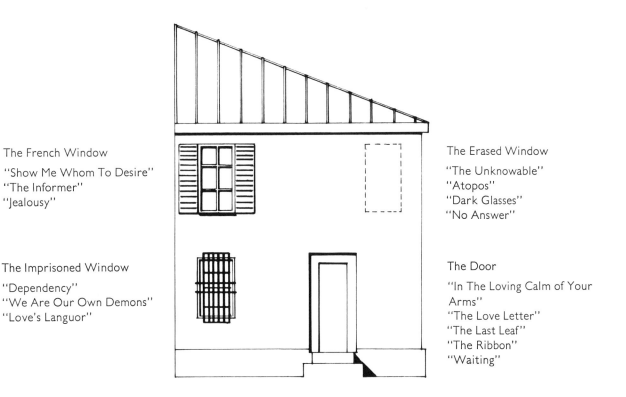

The French Window

"Show Me Whom To Desire"
"The Informer"
"Jealousy"

The Erased Window

"The Unknowable"
"Atopos"
"Dark Glasses"
"No Answer"

The Imprisoned Window

"Dependency"
"We Are Our Own Demons"
"Love's Languor"

The Door

"In The Loving Calm of Your Arms"
"The Love Letter"
"The Last Leaf"
"The Ribbon"
"Waiting"

Finally, the *Door*: "In the Loving Calm of Your Arms," "The Love Letter," "The Last Leaf," "The Ribbon," "Waiting." "I have received orders not to move." The ultimate yes or no, either open or closed, either home or gone.

Behind the Love Wall, love may ultimately be consummated, but it is waiting that permeates his site, a tension that establishes a bondage between him and her house. His love/her house: Love/House. He cannot move.

He stands in his own dream. Reality surrounds him. Her house: his consciousness. The widow's house: her fate? The school behind her house: his knowledge. The madman's ragged house: his fate? The immigrants to his side: his fate too. The Unknown behind him: everyone's fate. His Dream Machine: his consciousness embedded in its particular reality (madness, widowhood, knowledge,

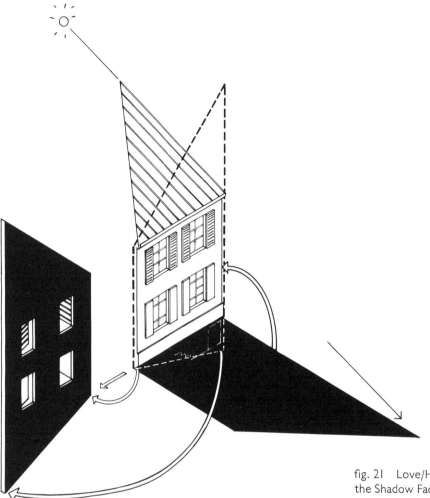

fig. 21 Love/House: The Construction of the Shadow Facade (Erection-Turn-Shift)

otherness, the unknown) separated from the site of his dream house by a chasm, a distance, a slash: Freud's preconscious, which "like a screen stands between consciousness and the unconscious." This void is the extension of the central path that connects the four courts to the city—now the path to the unconscious.

Parallel to her side facade, he erects Freud's screen: the first wall in the dream house. Her house/the void between/his future house—the tripartite figure. The transformation can begin.

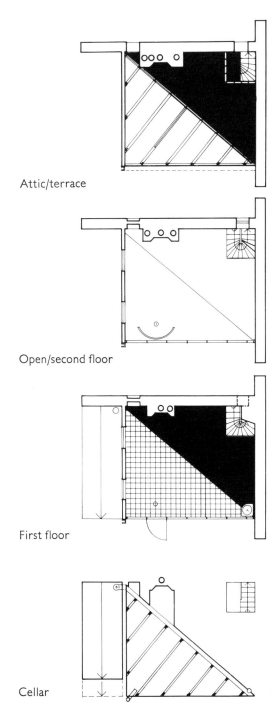

Attic/terrace

Open/second floor

First floor

Cellar

fig. 22 Love/House: Plans

Transformations

A house of shadows, a dream house never to be built, a place for the imagination: such is the scaffold for the waiting lover. Dreams and architecture; curiously similar. The architect-lover dreams in images, not language. Language appears in footnotes, slogans, captions, all ready-made in consciousness. In the upside-down world of the dream, things, gestures, processes create enigmatic narratives open only to the most tentative of interpretations. It appears that dreams are transformations of consciousness. Freud's displacements and condensations, shifts of meaning and form between the waking world and the dream world: these are the rhetoric of dreams. Similarly, architecture is the transformation of an existing reality (her house), along channels such as those in Freud's dream machine: the rhetoric of architecture.

The first transformation: The shadow of her house, cast at his feet in the court, is raised, turned, and shifted across to his site to complete the first outlines of his house: the Screen, the Shadow Facade, the Wall to the Unknown, the Wall to the Others, the ground, and the sky. The shadow of her house, cast in the court, is the first and most fundamental transformation. The shadow cast by an object in the path of the sun is the primary conversion of that object. Converting "her" shadow into a house in which he waits is the thought that motivates the project. Tall, black, the shadow facade is the reduction of the thickness of her house into an outline: a figure of the figure. The windows are repeated, serving as the axis of conversion. The shutters are hung on the inside since, in the transformation (erection-turn-shift), the front has been turned outside-in to face him.

The plans—cellar, first floor, second floor, attic—correspond in location both in "plan" and in section, but in the transfer, internal transformations of their form and meaning have taken place.

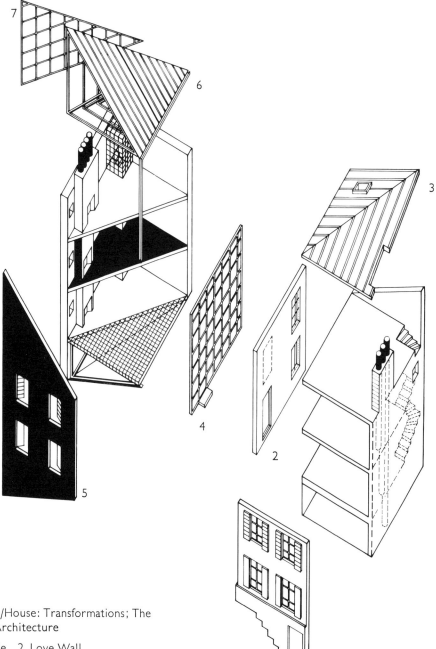

fig. 23   Love/House: Transformations; The
Rhetoric of Architecture

1. Front facade   2. Love Wall
3. Roof with suggested cut and skylight
4. Screen   5. Shadow facade   6. Cut roof
7. Giant window

Her roof has a diagonal break, suggesting that it could be cut in two; this cut is actually performed in his house. The dream house fulfills the fear. Half of his house is missing, the half he is waiting for: the better half. His house, a shadow of hers, has no content. The act of severing has emptied his house. Each floor, as well as the roof, the attic, and the cellar, have been affected by the cut.

Her cellar is dark and dank, filled with debris and the smell of the soil of the city. Her attic is warm and light and contains her bedroom. Half of his cellar is unexcavated, returned to the soil of the city. Correspondingly, half of his attic is turned into an open-air terrace: returned to the elements. In contrast to hers, the excavated half-cellar is made light by a glass-block floor above, and is made dry by covering the floor of the cellar with metal roofing. A reminder of her cellar's dankness, however, occurs every time it rains: the runoff water from the roof drains over the sloped floor of the cellar into one of its corners. The cellar is both cellar and anti-roof.

The half-attic next to his terrace has a sloping roof: her roof. The resulting large triangular wall between the terrace and his attic is made of glass. A giant window: her skylight. When he ascends the stairs and steps out on the cold and wet terrace and looks into his attic—her attic—there is no floor, no bed. There is no place for her in his house. The diabolical half-house is both inside-out/upside-down and beside itself: beside her house.

She has a dark room on the first floor: his corresponding half-room is black. She has a bright room on the second floor: his half-room is white. The screen wall floods his house with light: the room that should be dark is now just black; the room that should be bright is now bright and white. Shifts of value: dark to black. Amplification of value: bright to bright/white. This is the rhetoric of architecture.

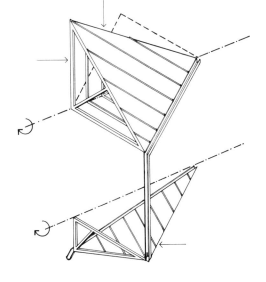

fig. 24   Love/House: Roof/Anti-roof

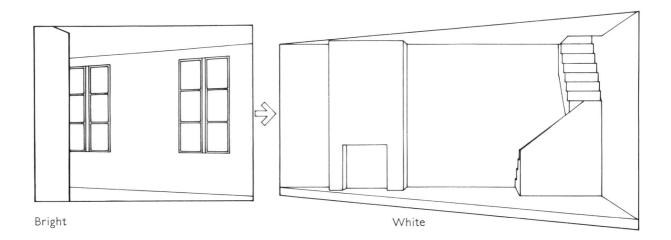

Bright

White

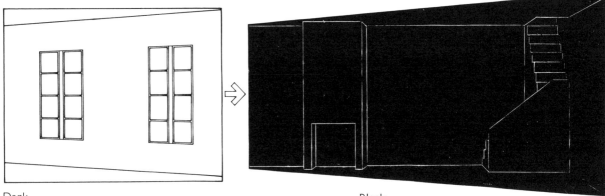

Dark

Black

fig. 25 Love/House: Rooms

There is a solitary window in the wall between her house and the schoolyard below. She can see the children at play: a monocular view of the observable. His corresponding wall is to the Unknown. Her window is projected onto his wall, repeated to provide a multitude of views. Each window is also transformed: open, closed, gridded, white, black, extruded, planned, and erased. Form over purpose. One can never know the unknown: windows must be open to all possibilities.

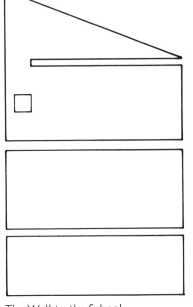

The Wall to the School

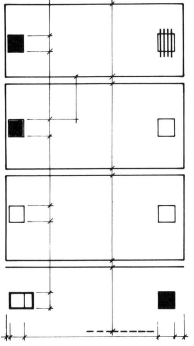

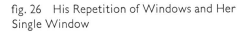

The Wall to the Unknown

fig. 26 His Repetition of Windows and Her
Single Window

Typically, the stair in the one-room plan of her house is located in a corner. U-shaped, it completes a half-turn at each floor. The fireplace is on the wall between her and the school, a second one on the floor above. The two flues are brought together in a chimney with a third flue from an abandoned fireplace in the cellar.

The stair in his house is in the corresponding corner but it has been rotated, so that the climber must adjust himself somewhat awkwardly to begin his climb: he must pay attention. An extra flight is added to a wine cellar below.

The stair to the wine cellar is made of heavy glass block; the one to the second floor is made of wood and black marble; the third flight is made of light, white wood. Finally, on the terrace a glass box caps the opening in the floor for the emerging white stair. The logic of this construction, which lightens with elevation, is the obverse of his experience, since he feels heavier as he climbs.

The chimney fulfills what has been prefigured in her chimney: now there is a fireplace on each floor, and the chimney stack becomes thicker and heavier as it rises. Logic over convention: the chimney appears upside down.

The dream house shows no mercy for the lover. Where is she? Will she ever come? With whom is she? Does she still love him? His endless questions are transformed through the rhetoric of the architecture/dream into images with their own logic and narrative power.

The dream is complete. The scaffold of waiting is constructed. Night turns into day: thick darkness into sharp shadow. With a simple pull at the syntactic string, the scaffold is involved in its own transformation. The logic of shadows, its props and crutches, is exposed to the amnesia of the day.

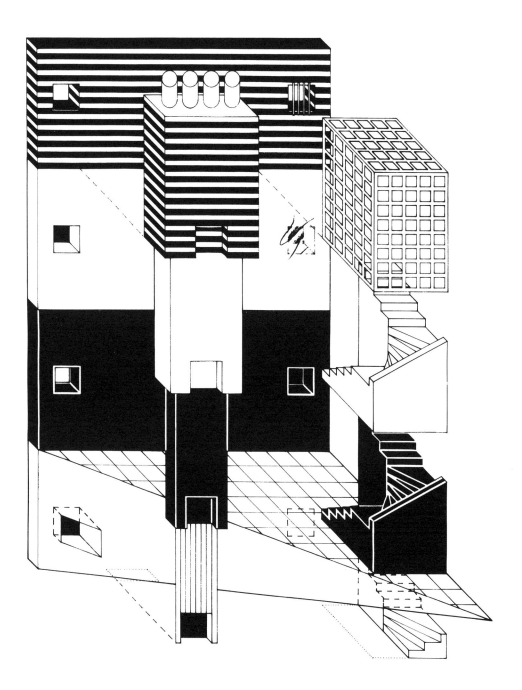

fig. 27   Love/House: Chimney and Stair

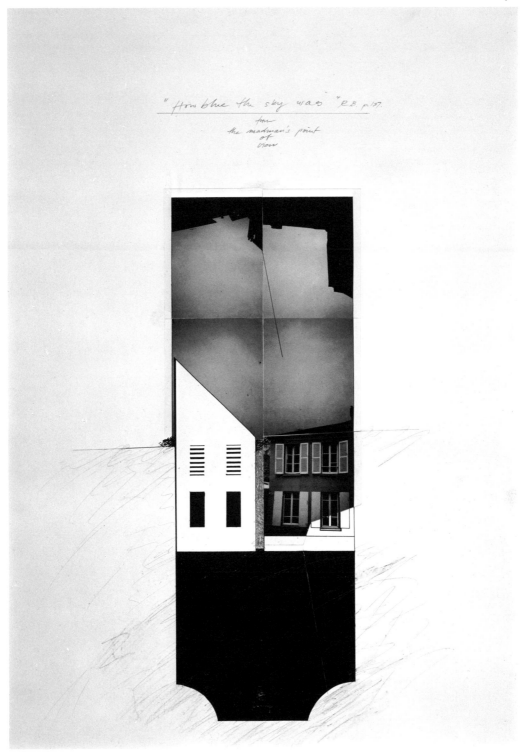

fig. 28 "How Blue The Sky Was": From the Madman's Point of View

He used to toss bundles of crumpled-up paper down into the court, come down the stairs, pick up the bundle, and twirl around with it in his arms, thus seeing the entire horizon of the court in one swoop.

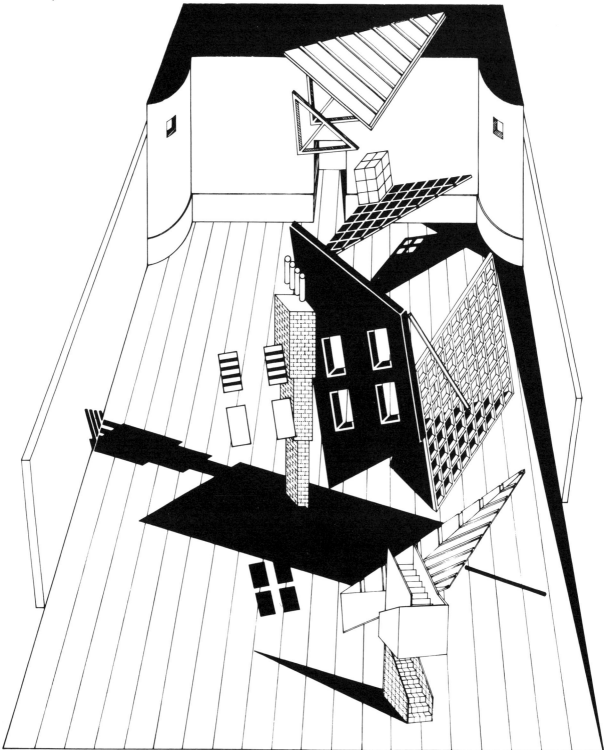

fig. 29 Love/House: The Final Transformation

fig. 30   The Almost Found Object

Texas Zero

The Broken Figure

The house is placed at the edge of an open expanse and a stand of liveoaks, above a meandering river in central Texas.

The building appears to be in the process of construction or possibly demolition. The large front facade leans outward, stabilized by wooden struts. The chimneys lean, ready to go up or down. The assembled familiar pieces are loosely fitted together: tentatively, even timidly. At the same time, the house appears finished, as if the construction process has been stopped and the builder, like a good *bricoleur*, has remedied the unfinishedness by shrouding it in finishing touches. In fact, these finishings serve as a veil, what the Greeks called the *parergon*, the by-work, covering, but separate from, the real work, the *ergon*, or structure behind. Here, however, the veil works the other way around: the by-work has become the work, covering an incompleteness. The outer appearance is the structure that holds the pieces together.

The finishing helps the house to look like a house, a jumble of things hidden under a veneer. But why all these tricks and machinations?

We have come to realize that meaning is both willed and unwilled; the relationship between meaning and object is forever ambiguous. We may act as though nothing has happened, and the house will continue to serve as a mere backdrop, a machine to facilitate our daily lives. We may, on the other hand, take the opportunity to overcome the conventions of everyday life and allow the new wilderness to enter. This is the place for Texas Zero.

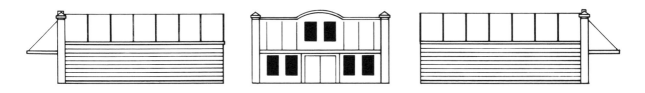

fig. 31   The Country Store: Elevations,
View, Plan, and Elements

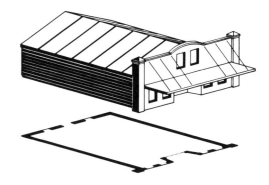

Children possess an astonishing ability to endow with life such apparently inanimate objects as teddy bears. The teddy bear is a model of a bear. Its "life" is willed and powerful. The Texas Zero is not a model of a house, but it is not quite a house either, because of the breaks in its image. The breaks make it accessible to the imagination. The spell of the figure is broken. Like the model of the bear, its reality is in question; it needs to be acted upon.

The client needs a place of her own. She wants her independence; she has been a wife and a mother for a long time. She needs a refuge, a place to hide, a domain where she can guide meaning and invent a world that is her own.

Antecedents

The Texas cultural landscape is dotted with reminders of its past: towns, stores, houses, streets, and squares. They bespeak a history of ingenuity and determination that has resulted in simple and beautiful everyday objects whose origins are not yet forgotten. These type-objects still have a place in modern Texas.

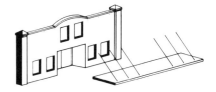

The typical country store with a grand facade facing the street, pragmatically slapped onto a loft space in the rear, provides the initial inspiration for the house. The facade is

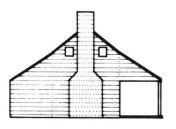
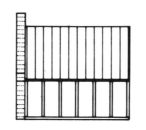
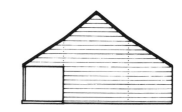

fig. 32   The Texas Log House: Elevations, View, Plan, and Elements

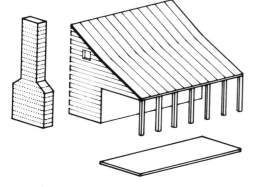

a sign, both inviting and protecting, even a pretence. It prefigures the modern billboard, but here the message and the structure—the supporting pylons—have been separated.

Through the now familiar conversion, Texas Zero begins with a facsimile of the grand store facade, reduced and conceived as a wall of glass block—both a facade and a giant window. The entry canopy becomes the carport. A fake door—a trompe-door—is placed in the centre to complete the reduction and to suggest the obvious (not-actual) place of entry. The facade becomes a wall of protection; its apparently but not actually precarious lean is a reminder of the most fundamental precondition of building—gravity.

The other found object is the Texas log house. Its history is long and complex. A particular house is chosen, cut in half, and simply attached to the back of the giant facade. Initially, the pieces of the house are left intact: the chimney, a simple rectangular box for the house, a "Louisiana"-type roof, and a porch. All the architect needs to know about its history is written in the house itself, in its simple elements and their distribution. This is the power of conventions.

The Plan

A tripartite figure formed of two small houses, separated by an open loft space, is held together by the frame of the giant front facade. Two single-family house figures, half a Texas log house, and a store front complete an almost found object. A break in a continuous closet behind the facade establishes the beginning of an axis, with the trompe-door at one end and a porch at the other. This axis propels the transformation of the entire plan.

On one side is a small black concrete house, completely occupied by a kitchen. Its counterpart is the opposite house, which contains the bathroom. The symmetrical placement of washbasin and kitchen sink, toilet and stove, bathtub and dishwasher, imply equivalences despite obvious differences. The ambiguity that results from the potential confusion between washing one's face and washing one's plate provides the key to Texas Zero's wilderness: the owner must decide for herself what it all means.

The two black houses are models of the typical house. They are also rooms housing the kitchen and bath—the only rooms left from the typical house. From the outside they may appear as models of the single-family house, but from the inside they are only fragments of the whole. The house is the bath, the kitchen is the house.

A series of reversions is employed. First, a leaning fireplace in compression, a sofa that is also a bed, and another leaning fireplace in tension are lined up on a secondary axis that is perpendicular to the main axis. As in Bertie Wooster's "He has, has he?" a reversal of meaning takes place. There, through the use of symmetry around the comma, the statement of fact "He has" is put in question by the syntactical reversion "has he?" In the Texas Zero, the reversion has a fundamental effect on the whole sentence. The very stability of the chimneys and the sofa (bed) has been put in question. Yet their instability is only apparent and serves to reveal the source of their stability. The struts and

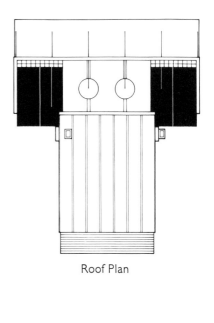

Roof Plan

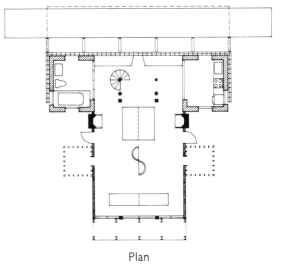

Plan

fig. 33   Texas Zero: Plans

pl. 33   Texas Zero: Leaning Front Facade, Leaning Fireplaces, and Truss

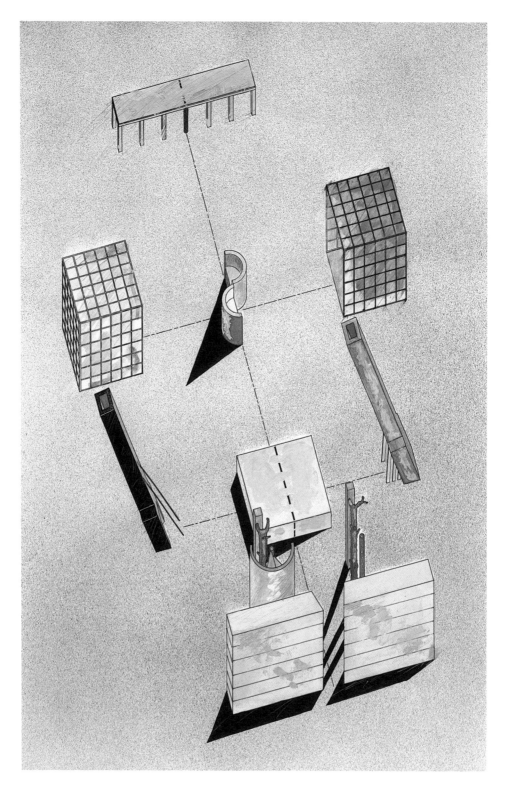

pl. 34   Texas Zero: Axes of Furniture

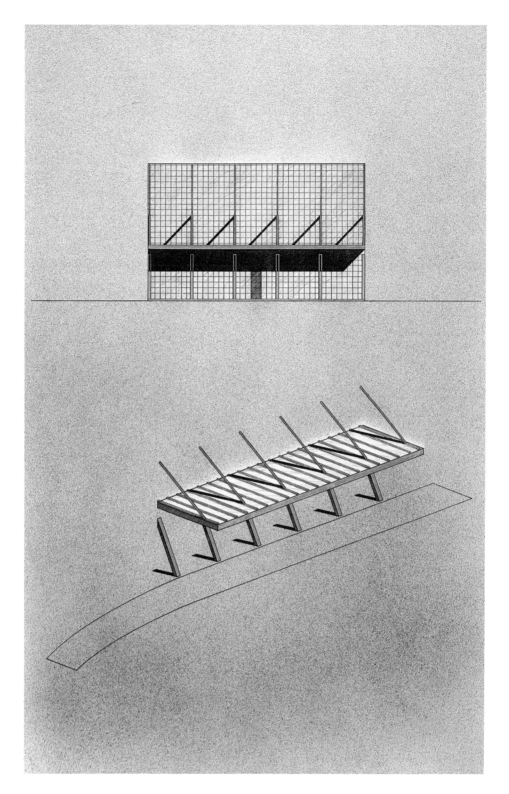

pl. 35   Texas Zero: North Facade and Canopy

pl. 36   Texas Zero: The Blue View; Perspective from Northwest

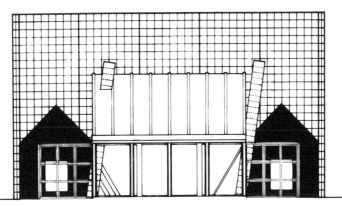

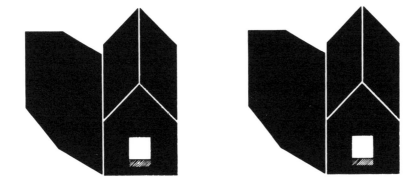

fig. 34   Texas Zero: South Facade, Bath and Kitchen Houses

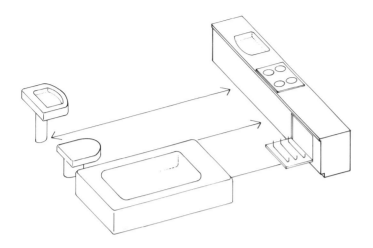

fig. 35   Texas Zero: Axis of Equipment

tension wires reveal and figure the presence of gravity, and the marriage of sofa and bed reveals their (un)comfortable similarity. The nature of things is displayed on their surface. Their place in the everyday narrative is exposed; names recede in favour of a literal representation of structure and form.

The roof trusses display the same clarity of conception and construction. Wires and I-beams are used for the structural members in tension, timber and lumber for members in compression. Revealed behaviour of structure makes the conventions of construction ambiguous. The reversion leads the eye back to the mechanics of trusses, away from the place of the truss in the periphery of the narrative.

A sleeping porch, essential during the hot summer months, is balanced symmetrically by a gilded cage for a pair of doves. Both cages are faced by the Which-Way Chair. Her decision.

The Last Supper Table (she always says, "this is the last supper I will serve") is a place both to eat and to work. When she works (and drinks) she is "above" the table. Out on the porch for fresh air, she is "under" the table: the porch is a giant replica of the Last Supper Table.

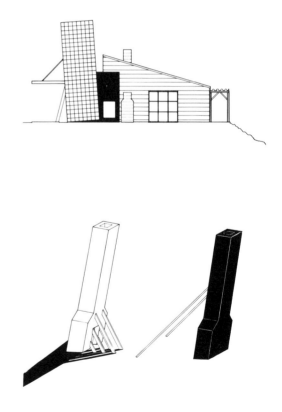

fig. 36   Texas Zero: West Facade and Leaning Fireplaces

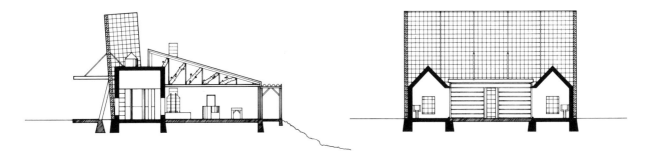

fig. 37   Texas Zero: Sections

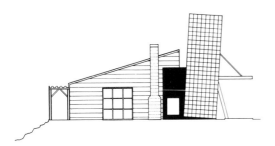

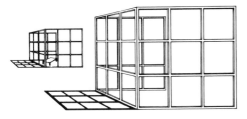

fig. 38   Texas Zero: East Facade, Sleeping Porch, and Gilded Cage

The result is a plan degree zero. By removing the syntax of the single-family house and replacing its narrative order—garage, living room, dining room, kitchen, hallway, master bedroom, master bath—and its additional subassemblies of rooms with a complete set of symmetries, the ground of the common elements has been neutralized, familiar as they are, and importantly so, the elements, freed from conventional use, gain new significance and an openness to interpretation and appreciation. When their names are removed, their forms come forth. Although they retain some of their old meaning, a new order is imposed through axiality and symmetry. The tension between the old meaning and the new order creates a status quo, where names and uses are no longer the primary force in establishing meaning.

The Texas Zero stands at the junction between vernacular tradition, steeped in conventions, and architectural materialism, where we begin the transformation with conventions rather than geometry, and where functionalism is undermined by function, form by material, structure by construction, space by place. The new house must function not for the mythical family but personally and architecturally—a new wilderness in which architectural form is given a privileged status.

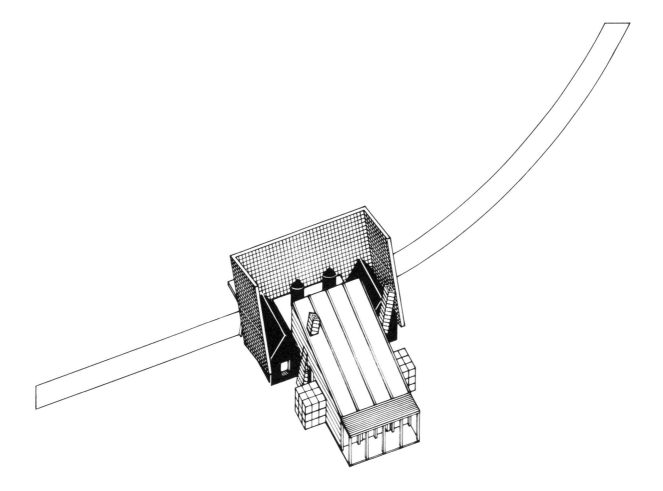

fig. 39   Texas Zero

Postscript

Text as Zero:
Or: The Destruction of Narrative

Today simulation, the simulacrum of what was formerly "real," has erased the opposition between reality and fiction. Whereas before, fiction (representation) simulated the real, and thus followed from it, now it is the real which simulates and follows from fiction.

To understand this phenomenon one has only to watch a presidential news conference to see a president being "presidential," that is, acting as he is told he is supposed to be, rather than being as he is. Or, similarly, to watch the performance of the "winning coach" affecting the reality of a winner in a post-game interview. Or consider the "reality" of a live horse race at a racetrack where much of the race is obscured by a giant television screen showing a simulcast of what it is obscuring. In each situation "reality" becomes a simulation or a *framing* of a simulation.

In his film *Zelig*, Woody Allen uses the inevitable exhaustion which occurs when a simulation can (because of sheer technical capacity) be made to be indistinguishible from reality as a frame for criticism. The film simulates a "real" biography of a man called Zelig, and it is through the use of its framing mechanism—that is, by putting quotation marks around this seeming reality—that Allen is able to return the film to a fiction, one which at that point becomes critical of its own simulation, that is, it becomes a framing within a framing.

In architecture, postmodernism, rather than confronting this crisis of reality, becomes a participant in it by a framing of its own. But unlike the self-criticism of Woody Allen's film, postmodernism exhibits a failure to be critical. It posits the frame as a mask, as a dissimulation, which says "this is not reality." What postmodernism does not add, which is its implicit message and which would be its critical gesture, is that this "not reality" is all that is left of the reality of architecture.

The postmodernists put their dissimulations forward as an authentic architecture, but they can be seen as another kind of framing: a fiction which is not critical of architecture, which does not acknowledge its own unreality. It is not that their architecture becomes unreal, for it does not surrender its own metaphysic; rather architecture becomes meta-theatre, the art of the giant stage set. When, for example, a Michael Graves uses "papier-mâché" keystones such as the one for the Portland Building, or a Robert Venturi paints the words "William and Mary" on a cartooned version of the original piece of furniture, these cry out, "This is not-reality." They are in fact the residue of a former and now empty reality. They speak of the impossibility of reuniting Foucault's figuration and discourse (facture and meaning) in a relativistic world where reality no longer exists as such but only as a parody of its former self.

As dissimulation is the last tactic of relativism, it also is the initial strategy of the absolutist. It is in this context that the stage set houses of Lars Lerup sound a similar chorus. To begin, for Lerup, is to frame existence. By saying, "This is not reality; this is a dream, or a shadow," is to begin with an abdication placed in a stage set storefront to nothingness. By violently framing or de-framing (even de-faming) the traditional metaphysics of an anthropocentric architecture—the mimetic conventions of narrative, of use, of site, of vertebrate structure—Lerup attempts to recapture a "former" architecture that, because it never was, can never be.

Here he consciously traps us in the futility of a paradox. He asks the question: in the world as simulation, where there is and can be no "reality," how can there be a "representation of reality," that is, what was formerly known as architecture? Thus his narrative emerges as a text on the emptiness of the classical architectural text; his architecture stands perpetually deferred from and expectant of its own mute dreams—an architecture degree zero, but not a tabula rasa: a de(sign). A sign of its own silence and displacement, it becomes a site for potential meaning.

Unlike Graves's or Venturi's historicizing figures, which attempt to gain value from a dissimulation of history, Lerup's dissimulations have figure but no figural value: they remain within the architectural metaphysic of shelter, definition and habitation, without deploying these for their symbolic value. They are text as zero. But they are no longer literal objects any more than they are represented meanings. The old distinction between aesthetic object (the signified), and text (the signifier) is erased; objects and texts are now equivalent: objects mean and texts sensate. These are Lerup's "new sentences."

In an age of simulation perhaps the one remaining example of a vanishing authenticity is violence, the destruction of the 'frame,' the deframing of reference. For Lerup the text now becomes the assault, an authentically violent assault on the paradigm of "frame" itself, the stability of the metaphysic of "house." But it is no longer "house" as merely an object which is the locus of this violence but rather "house" as text. While architects such as Frank Gehry or Site Inc. *represent* destruction, their houses remain aesthetic objects rather than sites for reading. For Lerup, on the other hand, the process of the narrative becomes the axis of destruction.

In a way, Lerup's text houses remind one of John Hejduk's poetic and mystic notations. Hejduk's is a textuality which also attempts to break down anthropocentrism. His "houses" begin to look like prehistoric animals, his sites like the savannah of a mystical planet. While Hejduk's anamorphic creatures possess a primitive and furry warmth, Lerup's seemingly familiar objects become distant dream machines and cool dissimulations.

But for all this, Lerup's texts remain encumbered with a certain logocentrism in the form of a justification for this absent architecture. His texts continue to appeal to "the" correct reading, that is, to the intention of an author who himself can only be furthest away from knowing such a correctness.

It is this desire for correctness that reveals in Lerup a nostalgia for the "aura" of the absolute, for that which is real. Lerup becomes symptomatic of the current state of modernity: an absolutist knowing himself to be inescapably caught within and at the same time compelled to escape from anthropocentric paradigms (particularly from the classical paradigm of the absolute). Lerup, who believes in the avant garde, can thus only dissimulate as a displacement of Platonic idealism. It is only in the desire for the authority of the athentic that the drive of man to transcend man, to distinguish music from noise, poetry from reportage, and meaning from gibberish can produce an *other* text, a text which attempts to elude the closure of anthropocentrism, without being thematic of another centrism.

For example, Lerup's text makes an initial attempt to leave anthropocentrism in the tripartite symmetry of Love/House. In its triadic structure Lerup intends to echo the psychological structure: unconscious, preconscious, conscious. However, the unconscious and the conscious are not opposites which can be reflected in a tripartite symmetry of presence. The unconscious is essential absence, which can only be "traced" in presence. Presence therefore is no longer whole; it can no longer account for all that is real.

Equally, Lerup's modern androgynous "person" is no longer whole. While sexuality can be simulated and conflated the psyche and the ego cannot. Today's "people" may be physically the same size as our former male husbands and female wives, but the comfortable illusion of these figures as mentally the same has been blown apart. The architectural needs of today's "people" are fundamentally in question. No longer is the mimesis of their vertebrate structure in the image of the central hearth sufficient to sustain the concept of *house*. No longer is the representation of their union sustained under one gabled roof. The grand abstraction of man as the measure of all things can no longer be maintained. Before Freud, man knew himself inasmuch as he was present to himself, inasmuch as he felt himself to be. After Freud's exposition of the unconscious, this naive anthropocentrism was rendered untenable. Hence the shadow houses of Lerup's work; they attempt to remake the unconscious. They represent as much a despair for reality as a concern for the unconscious.

Unlike Roland Barthes, who has written that "the text needs its shadow," Lerup makes the text a shadow, both as the unconscious and as a mask, a dissimulation that says, "I am not conscious, I am not real." The remaking of the unconscious in Lerup's Love/House is one example of a dissimulation that contains the masking of conscious reality. This masking is a walk through Lerup's own life, and it is here that the genuine desire for an authentic architecture is wedded to a nostalgia for a real Lerup. His nostalgia for the sensuality and comfort of symmetry is seen in his drawings, which reveal, like the sexual organs of an androgynous plastic human torso, a Dionysian who subsumes the classical aesthetic value of that same symmetry— not as an aesthetic object but in the violent deconstruction of the rationality of process. In Lerup's writings there is a nostalgia for a lost Eden in such phrases as "logical integral clarity" or "text as zero," the "zero degree" plan as the "new wilderness." *Alienation* is formed in the "axis of equipment," and *redemption* is desired in the "new significance." However, in the return to the aura of the authentic, in the replacement by one narrative of another, Lerup slips back into his own tendentious autobiography.

Because he is not able to distance himself totally from his classical background, Lerup's architectural graphs remain anthropocentric: chimneys as vertebrate symmetries, floor plans as horizontal ground datums, all measures of anthropocentrism. The metaphysics of plan conventions that he abandons in the Nofamily House and Love / House are also abandoned in the section of Texas Zero, but there the abandonment is violated by a new anthropomorphism. It is Lerup's aesthetic predilection for tripartite (closed, hierarchical, static) classicism which intrudes on his argument.

While Lerup desires to replace the narrative of man with the narrative of architecture, ultimately his architectural replacement remains, in its anthropocentrism, tied to man. However, it is in figure 29, "The Final Transformation," that Lerup's assault finally emerges most vigorously in his architecture. The fragments are at last cut loose from their anthropocentric spine, from their own aesthetic and figural objecthood. They are now but graphic counters, the traces of a process, and as such violent to the idea of centre, of spine, and of wholeness and enclosure.

In a world of simulation it is the authentic violence of process which supplants the futile nostalgia for the aura of the authentic object. This is the last critique by architecture of its own discourse. This, then, is the only authentic reality: the insatiable desire for the absolute. As such, it cannot be known, cannot be achieved; it can only be dreamed for. For Lerup it is not enough to be critical; one senses that it is now time for him to propose. Lerup's houses dream this.

Peter Eisenman

Sources

Before the beginning, there was Ulf Linde's *Spejare: En Essä om Konst* (Sentinel: An essay on art; Stockholm, 1961), which I read in 1973. Linde opened the door to "the engaged reading," Marcel Duchamp, and the role of the spectator in synthesizing the art object.

On the notion of "beginning" and "the beginning," essential for understanding the modernist refusal to acknowledge the past, see Edward W. Said, *Beginnings: Intention and Method* (New York: Basic Books, 1975). On the role of the family and its source of power, in particular the notion of a "disciplinary mechanism," see Michel Foucault, *Discipline and Punish: The Birth of the Prison* (New York: Pantheon Books, 1977), as well as his *History of Sexuality,* volume 1, *An Introduction* (New York: Pantheon Books, 1978).

The ideas of the assault on the referent (the family in this case) and of the secondary status of the built as the vehicle of referentiality—the underpinnings of the entire project—are inspired by Jacques Derrida's *Of Grammatology* (Baltimore and London: The Johns Hopkins University Press, 1976). The notions of erasure, insertion, figure/form, and montage (according to which the figure of the house must be present in order to unsettle its dominance) are all Derridean concepts. On the obsession with language and its hegemony over our existence see Jacques Lacan, "The Insistence of the Letter in the Unconscious," in *Structuralism,* ed. Ehrman (New York: Anchor Books, 1970). The literary inspiration for the Love/House is Roland Barthes's *The Lover's Discourse: Fragments,* trans. Richard Howard (New York: Hill and Wang, 1978; translation © 1969 by Farrar, Straus and Giroux, Inc.). All quotations are from this edition. The notion of the dream technology comes from Sigmund Freud, *The Interpretation of Dreams* (New York: Avon Books, 1965). All quotations are from this edition. Among other writers and artists whose work provided inspiration are Giorgio de Chirico, René Magritte, Marcel Duchamp, Stéphane Mallarmé, and Jorge Luis Borges, who wrote in *The Immortal* (1949), "Stairs would die without leading anywhere."

Figures and Plates

Credits

Figs. 1, 2, 4, 5, and 10 are reproductions of works not by the author.

The drawings in fig. 1 are stock plans for two different houses. Fig. 2 is a collage from an advertisement. Fig. 5 is a collage from an advertisement for Carrier air conditioners. The author regrets that he no longer has complete information about the sources of these images.

Fig. 4 is a photograph by David Hanawalt, Berkeley, California (reproduced by permission of the photographer).

Fig. 10 reproduces an illustration from *Marcel Duchamp* (exhibition catalogue), ed. Anne d'Harnoncourt and Kynaston McShine (New York: Museum of Modern Art/New York Graphic Society, 1973). Copyright 1973 The Museum of Modern Art, New York. All rights reserved; reprinted by permission. Marcel Duchamp's *Trebuchet* (Trap), second version, is in the Mary Sisler Collection.

Dimensions are given in centimetres, height times width.

All drawings are by Lars Lerup.

Abbreviations:
CCA = Centre Canadien d'Architecture/ Canadian Centre for Architecture, Montréal
LL = Lars Lerup, Berkeley

Figures

fig. 3 *Nofamily House, Love/ House, and Texas Zero: The Tripartite Figures* (1984). Black ink on vellum, 27.9 x 21.5. (LL)

fig. 6 *The Nofamily House: Zone of Passion* (1984). Black ink on vellum, 27.9 x 21.5. (LL)

fig. 7 *The Nofamily House: Eight-Degree Fissures* (1984). Black ink on vellum, 27.9 x 21.5. (LL)

fig. 8 *The Nofamily House: Plan 1* (1981). Black ink on vellum, 35.6 x 43.1. (CCA)

fig. 9 *The Nofamily House: Plan 2* (1981). Black ink on vellum, 35.6 x 43.1. (CCA)

fig. 11 *The Nofamily House: Section* (1981). Black ink on vellum, 35.6 x 43.1. (CCA)

fig. 12 *The Nofamily House: The Stair That Leads Nowhere* (1983). Black ink on vellum, 27.9 x 21.5. (LL)

fig. 13 *The Nofamily House: Front Facade; North* (1981). Black ink on vellum, 35.6 x 43.1. (CCA)

fig. 14 *The Nofamily House: Side Facade; East* (1981). Black ink on vellum, 35.6 x 43.1. (CCA)

fig. 15 *The Nofamily House: Back Facade; South* (1981). Black ink on vellum, 35.6 x 43.1. (CCA)

fig. 16 *The Nofamily House: Side Facade; West* (1981). Black ink on vellum, 35.6 x 43.1. (CCA)

fig. 17 *The Nofamily House: Axonometric from Under* (1981). Black ink on vellum, 35.6 x 43.1. (CCA)

fig. 18 *Love/House: The Fourth Court; Her House and Context* (1984). Black ink on vellum, 27.9 x 21.5. (LL)

fig. 19 *Love/House: Her House; Section* (1984). Black ink on vellum, 27.9 x 21.5. (LL)

fig. 20 *Love/House: The Love Wall; The Locus of Barthes's Amorous Figures* (1984). Black ink on vellum, 27.9 x 21.5. (LL)

fig. 21 *Love/House: The Construction of the Shadow Facade; Erection-Turn-Shift* (1983). Black ink on vellum, 27.9 x 21.5. (LL)

fig. 22 *Love/House: Plans* (1983). Black ink on vellum, 27.9 x 21.5. (LL)

fig. 23 *Love/House: Transformations; The Rhetoric of Architecture* (1984). Black ink on vellum, 27.9 x 21.5. (LL)

fig. 24 *Love/House: Roof/Anti-Roof* (1983). Black ink on vellum, 27.9 x 21.5. (LL)

fig. 25 *Love/House: Rooms* (1984). Black ink on vellum, 27.9 x 21.5. (LL)

fig. 26 *Love/House: His Repetition of Windows and Her Single Window* (1983). Black ink on vellum, 27.9 x 21.5. (LL)

fig. 27 *Love/House: Chimney and Stair* (1985). Black ink on vellum, 27.9 x 21.5. (LL)

fig. 28 *Love/House: "How Blue the Sky Was"; From the Madman's Point of View* (1982). Collage of Polaroid photographs, black ink, and graphite on white bristol board, 59 x 42. (LL)

fig. 29 *Love/House: The Final Transformation* (1984). Black ink on vellum, 27.9 x 21.5. (LL)

fig. 30 *Texas Zero: The Almost Found Object* (1984). Black ink on vellum, 27.9 x 21.5. (LL)

fig. 31 *Texas Zero: The Country Store; Elevations, View, Plan, and Elements* (1984). Black ink on vellum, 27.9 x 21.5. (LL)

fig. 32 *Texas Zero: The Texas Log House; Elevations, View, Plan, and Elements* (1984). Black ink on vellum, 27.9 x 21.5. (LL)

fig. 33 *Texas Zero: Plans* (1984). Black ink on vellum, 27.9 x 21.5. (LL)

fig. 34 *Texas Zero: South Facade and Bath and Kitchen Houses* (1984). Black ink on vellum, 27.9 x 21.5. (LL)

fig. 35 *Texas Zero: Axis of Equipment* (1984). Black ink on vellum, 27.9 x 21.5. (LL)

fig. 36 *Texas Zero: West Facade and Leaning Fireplaces* (1984). Black ink on vellum, 27.9 x 21.5. (LL)

fig. 37 *Texas Zero: Sections* (1984). Black ink on vellum, 27.9 x 21.5. (LL)

fig. 38 *Texas Zero: East Facade, Sleeping Porch, and Gilded Cage* (1984). Black ink on vellum, 27.9 x 21.5. (LL)

fig. 39 *Texas Zero: View* (1984). Black ink on vellum, 27.9 x 21.5. (LL)

Plates

pl. 1 *The Nofamily House: The Erasure of the Derelict House* (1980). Coloured pencil, graphite, ballpoint pen with red ink, and black ink on white bristol board, 27.9 x 21.5. (CCA)

pl. 2 *The Nofamily House: The Glass House and Its Double* (1980). Coloured pencil, graphite, ballpoint pens with blue and red ink, and black ink on white bristol board, 27.9 x 21.5. (CCA)

pl. 3 *The Nofamily House: The Phantom's Fata Morgana or the Mad Swarming* (1980). Coloured pencil, graphite, ballpoint pens with blue and red ink, and black ink on white bristol board, 27.9 x 21.5. (CCA)

pl. 4 *The Nofamily House: The Insertion of Architecture* (1980). Coloured pencil, graphite, ballpoint pens with red and blue ink, and black ink on white bristol board, 27.9 x 21.5. (CCA)

pl. 5 *The Nofamily House: Sketch; Facade, Plan, Section, and View* (1979). Felt-tip pen with blue and red ink, coloured pencil, and graphite on yellow graph paper, 27.9 x 21.5. (CCA)

pl. 6 *The Nofamily House: Sketch; First Rotation* (1979). Coloured pencil, graphite, black ink, and masking tape on white paper, 27.9 x 21.5. (CCA)

pl. 7 *The Nofamily House: Preliminary Design; Fold-Out View* (1979). Coloured pencil, black ink, graphite, wax crayons, watercolour, and ballpoint pen with blue ink on white bristol board, 73.6 x 58.5. (CCA)

pl. 8 *The Nofamily House: Plan 1* (1980). Coloured pencil, graphite, and ballpoint pens with blue and red ink on white bristol board, 27.9 x 21.5. (CCA)

pl. 9 *The Nofamily House: Plan 2* (1980). Coloured pencil, graphite, and ballpoint pen with blue ink on white bristol board, 27.9 x 21.5. (CCA)

pl. 10 *The Nofamily House: Roof Plan* (1980). Coloured pencil, graphite, and ballpoint pens with blue and red ink on white bristol board, 27.9 x 21.5. (CCA)

pl. 11 *The Nofamily House: Site Plan* (1979). Coloured pencil, graphite, black ink, watercolour, wax crayons, and ballpoint pens with blue and red ink on white bristol board, 73.6 x 58.5. (CCA)

pl. 12 *The Nofamily House: A Stumble of Traps; The Liberated Handrail, the Useless Door, the Fresh Window, the Stair That Leads Nowhere* (1980). Coloured pencil, graphite, ballpoint pen with blue ink, and black ink on white bristol board, 27.9 x 21.5. (CCA)

pl. 13 *The Nofamily House: The Liberated Handrail* (1983). Airbrush, black ink, and coloured pencil over a blackline Xerox print on white paper, 43.1 x 27.9. (LL)

pl. 14 *The Nofamily House: The Useless Door* (1983). Airbrush, black ink, and coloured pencil over a blackline Xerox print on white paper, 43.1 x 27.9. (LL)

pl. 15 *The Nofamily House: The Fresh Window* (1983). Airbrush, black ink, coloured pencil, and attached postcard over a blackline Xerox print on white paper, 43.1 x 27.9. (LL)

pl. 16 *The Nofamily House: Interior Views; Perspective from Architecture's Point of View (Left)* (1980). Coloured pencil, graphite, black ink, wax crayons, watercolour, and ballpoint pens with blue and red ink on white bristol board, 76.2 x 50. (CCA)

pl. 17 *The Nofamily House: Interior Views; Perspective from Architecture's Point of View (Right)* (1980). Coloured pencil, graphite, black ink, watercolour, wax crayons, and ballpoint pen with blue ink on white bristol board, 76.2 x 50. (CCA)

pl. 18a *The Nofamily House: Dissection; The Locus of the Family* (1980). Coloured pencil, graphite, watercolour, wax crayons, and ballpoint pens with blue and red ink on white bristol board, 39.4 x 47. (CCA)

pl. 18b *The Nofamily House: Dissection; The Locus of Architecture (Inside)* (1980). Coloured pencil, graphite, watercolour, wax crayons, and black ink on white bristol board, 39.4 x 47. (CCA)

pl. 18c *The Nofamily House: Dissection; The Locus of Architecture (Outside)* (1980). Coloured pencil, graphite, watercolour, wax crayons, and black ink on white bristol board, 39.4 x 47. (CCA)

pl. 19   *The Nofamily House:
View* (1980). Coloured pencil, graphite, black ink, and
ballpoint pens with blue and
red ink on white bristol
board, 27.9 x 21.5. (CCA)

pl. 20   *The Nofamily House:
Plan 3; With Glass Surfaces
Folded Out* (1980). Black ink,
coloured pencil, graphite,
and ballpoint pens with blue
and red ink on vellum,
68.6 x 61. (CCA)

pl. 21   *The Nofamily House:
Zone of Passion; Rotation and
Shift* (1980). Coloured pencil, graphite, black ink, and
ballpoint pens with blue
and red ink on white bristol
board, 27.9 x 21.5. (CCA)

pl. 22   *The Nofamily House:
Exploration; The Shafts of
Light* (1980). Felt-tip pen
with blue ink, coloured pencil, graphite, and black ink
on white paper, 27.9 x 21.5.
(CCA)

pl. 23   *The Nofamily House:
Exploration; The Granite
Shadow* (1981). Black ink,
coloured pencil, and watercolour on vellum fastened
with masking tape on white
paper, 27.9 x 21.5. (CCA)

pl. 24   *The Nofamily House:
Foxtrot Collage; Roof Plan and
Elevations* (1980). Manila folder;
pink, blue, green, and yellow
paper; gridded celluloid; and
ballpoint pen with blue ink
on white bristol board,
95.2 x 80. (CCA)

pl. 25   *Love/House: Site
(City, District, House)* (1984).
Watercolour on Arches
white paper, 58.4 x 36.8. (LL)

pl. 26   *Love/House: The
Fourth Court* (1982). Coloured pencil, gouache, and
black ink on white bristol
board, 59 x 42. (LL)

pl. 27   *Love/House: Scene;
The Four Courts and the Eiffel
Tower* (1982). Collage of
Polaroid photograph, black
ink, graphite, coloured pencil, and gouache on white
bristol board, 59 x 42. (LL)

pl. 28   *Love/House: Transformations; Night and Day*
(1984). Watercolour,
gouache, coloured pencil,
graphite, black ink, and ballpoint pens with blue and red
ink on white bristol board,
58.4 x 36.8. (LL)

pl. 29   *Love/House: Freud's
Dream Technology* (1984).
Airbrush, black ink, and
coloured pencil over a blackline Xerox print on white
paper, 43.1 x 27.9. (LL)

pl. 30   *Love/House: Waiting
(At the Door)* (1983). Coloured pencil, graphite, and
ballpoint pen with blue ink
on white bristol board,
73.6 x 51.8. (LL)

pl. 31   *Love/House: "Malicious Spying," from the Widow's
Point of View* (1982). Collage
of Polaroid photograph, black
ink, graphite, gouache, and
coloured pencil on white
bristol board, 59 x 42. (LL)

pl. 32   *Love/House: Amorous
Drift; Enigma of the Night
(Amnesia of the Day)* (1984).
Black ink, graphite, coloured
pencil, watercolour, gouache,
and ballpoint pen with blue
ink on white bristol board,
58.4 x 36.8. (LL)

pl. 33   *Texas Zero: Leaning
Front Facade, Leaning Fireplaces, and Truss* (1984).
Gouache, black ink, graphite,
and ballpoint pen with blue
ink on white bristol board,
43.1 x 27.9. (Jamileh Weber,
Zurich)

pl. 34   *Texas Zero: Axes of
Furniture* (1984). Airbrush,
gouache, and black ink over
a blackline Xerox print on
white paper, 43.1 x 27.9. (LL)

pl. 35   *Texas Zero: North Facade and Canopy* (1984). Airbrush, coloured pencil, and gouache on a blackline Xerox print on white paper, 43.1 x 27.9. (LL)

pl. 36   *Texas Zero: The Blue View; Perspective from North-west* (1984). Airbrush and gouache on white bristol board, 51.4 x 35.6. (LL)

About the Author

Lars Lerup's work has been exhibited in one-person shows in Berkeley, New York, San Francisco, Zurich, Berlin, and Stockholm, and as part of "Ornament in the Twentieth Century" at the Cooper-Hewitt Museum in New York. His drawings are included in private collections and in the collections of the Canadian Centre for Architecture. His first published house project was *Villa Prima Facie* (1978). He is also the author of *Building the Unfinished: Architecture and Human Action* (1977).

Lerup was born in Sweden in 1940. He is an architect and a faculty member of the Department of Architecture, University of California, Berkeley, where he has taught since 1970.